THE
CULTURE
CODE

AN INGENIOUS WAY TO
UNDERSTAND WHY PEOPLE
AROUND THE WORLD BUY
AND LIVE AS THEY DO

Clotaire Rapaille

BROADWAY BOOKS · NEW YORK

PUBLISHED BY BROADWAY BOOKS

Copyright © 2006 by Clotaire Rapaille
Afterword copyright © 2007 by Clotaire Rapaille

A hardcover edition of this book was originally published in 2006 by Broadway.

Published in the United States by Broadway Books, an imprint of
The Doubleday Broadway Publishing Group, a division of Random House, Inc., New York.

www.broadwaybooks.com

BROADWAY BOOKS and its logo, a letter B bisected on the diagonal,
are trademarks of Random House, Inc.

This title may be purchased for business or promotional use or for special sales.
For information, please write to: Special Markets Department, Random House, Inc.,
1745 Broadway, MD 6-3, New York, NY 10019, or specialmarkets@randomhouse.com.

Library of Congress Cataloging-in-Publication Data
Rapaille, Clotaire.
  The culture code: an ingenious way to understand why people around the world
buy and live as they do / by Clotaire Rapaille.
    p. cm.
Includes index.
  1. Social perception. 2. Cognition and culture. 3. National characteristics.
4. Consumer behavior—Psychological aspects. I. Title.

HM1041.R37 2006
305.8—dc22
2005058128

ISBN 978-0-7679-2057-5

PRINTED IN THE UNIED STATES OF AMERICA

10 9 8 7 6 5 4 3 2 1

First Paperback Edition

THE
CULTURE
CODE

This book is dedicated to the GI who gave me chocolate and chewing gum on top of his tank two weeks after D-Day . . . and changed my life forever.

One of the handicaps of the twentieth century is that we still have the vaguest and most biased notions, not only of what makes Japan a nation of Japanese, but of what makes the United States a nation of Americans, France a nation of Frenchmen, and Russia a nation of Russians . . . . Lacking this knowledge, each country misunderstands the other.
—Ruth Benedict, *The Chrysanthemum and the Sword*

We are all puppets, and our best hope for even partial liberation is to try to decipher the logic of the puppeteer.
—Robert Wright, *The Moral Animal*

CONTENTS

INTRODUCTION

For Americans, it's a gallop. For Europeans, it's a march. For Jeep, it was a breakthrough.

In the late 1990s, the Jeep Wrangler was struggling to regain its place in the American market. Once in a category all its own, it had been supplanted by scores of SUVs, most of which were bigger, more luxurious, and better suited to soccer moms. Chrysler had reached a crossroads with the Wrangler and gave serious thought to a major overhaul.

When I began working with Chrysler on the Jeep Wrangler in the late 1990s, the company's management was understandably suspicious about my approach to learning consumer preferences. They'd done extensive market research and had asked dozens of focus groups hundreds of questions. I walked through the door with a bunch of different approaches and they said to themselves, "What is this guy going to give us that we don't already have?"

The people at Chrysler had indeed asked hundreds of questions; they just hadn't asked the right ones. They kept listening to what people *said*. This is always a mistake. As a result, they had theories about moving the Wrangler in multiple directions (more luxurious, more like a traditional car, without removable doors, enclosed rather than convertible, and so on) with no clear path to follow. The Wrangler—the classic consumer Jeep—verged on losing its distinctive place in the universe of automobiles, becoming, for all intents and purposes, just another SUV.

When I put groups of consumers together, I asked them different questions. I didn't ask them what they wanted in a Jeep; I asked them to tell me about their earliest memories of Jeeps. Respondents told me hundreds of stories, and the stories had a strong recurring image—of being out on the open land, of going where no ordinary car could go, of riding free of the restraints of the road. Many people spoke of the American West or the open plains.

I returned to those wary Chrysler executives and told them that the Code for Jeep in America is HORSE. Their notion of turning the Wrangler into just another SUV was ill advised. SUVs are not horses. Horses don't have luxury appointments. Horses don't have butter-soft leather, but rather the tough leather of a saddle. The Wrangler needed to have removable doors and an open top because drivers wanted to feel the wind around them, as though they were riding on a horse.

The executives weren't particularly moved. After all, they had vast research that told them consumers said they wanted something else. Maybe people *once* thought of Jeeps as horses, but they didn't want to think of them that way any longer. I asked them to test my theory by making a relatively minor adjustment to the car's design: replacing the square headlights with round ones. Why? Because horses have round eyes, not square ones.

When it turned out that it was cheaper to build the car with round headlights, the decision became easier for them to make. They tested the new design and the response was instantly positive. Wrangler sales rose and the new "face" of the Wrangler became its most prominent and marketable feature. In fact, the car's logo has incorporated its grille and round headlights ever since. There are even Jeep fan clubs that distribute T-shirts to their members bearing the legend "Real Jeeps have round headlights."

Meanwhile, the company began to advertise the car as a "horse." My favorite ad shows a child in the mountains with a dog. The dog falls off a cliff and clings precariously to a tree. The kid runs into a nearby village for help. He passes sedans, minivans, and SUVs until he comes upon a Jeep Wrangler. The Wrangler scales the treacherous mountain terrain and its driver rescues the dog. The kid hugs the dog and then turns to thank the driver—but the Jeep is already heading back down the mountain, just like an old Western hero heading off into the sunset upon his steed. The campaign was a smash.

Bolstered by its American success, Chrysler hired me to discover the Code for the Wrangler in Europe. Respondents in both France and Germany saw Wranglers as reminiscent of the Jeeps American troops drove during World War II. For the French, this was the image of freedom from the Germans. For the Germans, this was the image of freedom from their darker selves. Repeatedly, the people in these countries told me stories about how the image of a Jeep gave them a sense of hope, reminding them of the end of difficult times and the dawn of better days. I returned to Chrysler and told them that the Code for the Jeep Wrangler in both countries was LIBERATOR.

With the news of the Code, Chrysler launched new campaigns in France and Germany. Here, though, instead of positioning the car as a horse, they stressed the Jeep's proud past and the freedom gained from driving a Wrangler. These campaigns were also tremendously successful, expanding market share for the Wrangler in both countries.

By this point, Chrysler's executives no longer doubted my approach. They'd come to appreciate the power of the Culture Code.

For Ritz-Carlton, the revelation came unexpectedly, via . . . toilet paper. When I began to consult for this company, I shocked them by telling them that the work they needed to do to improve customer satisfaction had to begin in the bathroom. Of course they thought I was delirious, but they heard me out.

If you ask most people why they buy the toilet paper they do, they will say, "Because it is soft and because it is on sale." They have no idea that the Code for toilet paper might be anything but strictly utilitarian. They are wrong. As with Jeep, my work with consumers to crack the Code for toilet paper revealed something powerful and unexpected about Americans' first imprint of a familiar product.

For American parents, toilet training is taken very seriously. For some, toilet training is considered so essential that they start the process not long after their child's first birthday. And, regardless of when they start, parents support a small industry of books, videos, and even psychologists who focus on the task. (A current controversy in the field involves the idea of the "diaper-free" baby, who may be toilet trained as early as eight months old!) Toilet training has significant social consequences: it affects everything from playdates to car trips to acceptance in preschool. There is also, of course, the stirring sense of liberation that comes when mothers and fathers realize they no longer need to change diapers.

For the American child himself, however, the completion of toilet training triggers a different response. Once he can use the toilet by himself—or, more specifically, use the toilet and *toilet paper* by himself—a remarkable thing happens. The child can now close the bathroom door, maybe even lock it, and *reject* his parents. And, amazingly, he will be praised for doing so. His parents are proud of him for not needing them anymore. They smile and applaud him. Sometimes they even buy him presents.

This imprint is fully associated with the use of toilet paper rather than the use of the toilet itself. In the early years, using the toilet still requires a parent to come in—or to sit there with the child until she is finished—to wipe up afterward. It is only after the child is adept at using toilet paper that she can be free behind the bathroom door. Free, and without guilt, since she has the full endorsement of the authority figures in her life.

This imprint is so strong in the American culture that the Culture Code for toilet paper is INDEPENDENCE.

For Ritz-Carlton, this meant a huge opportunity to cater to their guests in the one room of the house (or suite) that signifies complete privacy and independence. Why not have a phone in the bathroom? A notepad and pen to take notes? Why stop there—why not make the bathroom comfortable, spacious, and independent of the hotel suite? Merely functional, a bathroom is forgettable. A bathroom that is a fully equipped and independent retreat from the world, however, is right on Code. Indeed, if you look to the new homes being built in prosperous neighborhoods today, you will see the same effect. Bathrooms are growing ever larger, with formerly luxury appointments now standard—sunken bathtubs, double sinks, televisions, phone jacks, and always, always, a door to lock out the world.

The reason? The Codes.

The Culture Code is the unconscious meaning we apply to any given thing—a car, a type of food, a relationship, even a country—via the culture in which we are raised. The American experience with Jeeps is very different from the French and German experience because our cultures evolved differently (we have strong cultural memories of the open frontier; the French and Germans have strong cultural memories of occupation and war). Therefore, the Codes—the meanings we give to the Jeep at an unconscious level—are different as well. The reasons for this are numerous (and I will describe them in the next chapter), but it all comes down to the worlds in which we grew up. It is obvious to everyone that cultures are different from one another. What most people don't realize, however, is that these differences actually lead to our processing the same information in different ways.

My journey toward the discovery of cultural codes began in the early 1970s. I was a psychoanalyst in Paris at the time, and my clinical work brought me to the research of the great scientist Henri Laborit, who drew a clear connection between learning and emotion, showing that without the latter the former was impossible. The stronger the emotion, the more clearly an experience is learned. Think of a child told by his parents to avoid a hot pan on a stove. This concept is abstract to the child until he reaches out, touches the pan, and it burns him. In this intensely emotional moment of pain, the child learns what "hot" and "burn" mean and is very unlikely ever to forget it.

The combination of the experience and its accompanying emotion creates something known widely as an imprint, a term first applied by Konrad Lorenz. Once an imprint occurs, it strongly conditions our thought processes and shapes our future actions. Each imprint helps make us more of who we are. The combination of imprints defines us.

One of my most memorable personal imprints came when I was a young boy. I grew up in France, and when I was about four years old, my family received an invitation to a wedding. I'd never been to one before and I had no idea what to expect. What I encountered was remarkable. French weddings are unlike weddings in any other culture I know. The event went on for two days, nearly all of which was spent around a large communal table. People stood at the table to offer toasts. They climbed on the table to sing songs. They slept under the table and (as I later learned) even seduced one another under the table. Food was always available. People drank *le trou Normand,* a glass of Calvados that allowed them to make room for more food. Others simply went to the bathroom to vomit so they could eat more. It was an amazing thing for a child to see, and it left a permanent imprint on me. Forevermore, I would associate weddings with gustatory excess. In fact, the first time I went to a wedding in America, I was taken aback by how sedate it was in comparison. Recently, my wife (who also grew up in France) and I held the kind of multiday feast that meant "wedding" to both of us.

Every imprint influences us on an unconscious level. When the work of Laborit crystallized this for me, I began to incorporate what I had learned from him into my clinical work in Paris, most of which was being done with autistic children (in fact, Laborit led me to the theory that autistic children do not learn effectively because they lack the emotion to do so). The subject of imprinting also formed the foundation of the lectures I gave during this time. After one particular lecture at Geneva University, the father of a student approached me.

"Dr. Rapaille, I might have a client for you," he said.

Always intrigued at the possibilities offered by another case, I nodded with interest. "An autistic child?"

"No," he said, smiling. "Nestlé."

At the time, focused on clinical and scholarly work, I barely understood what the word "marketing" meant. I therefore couldn't possibly imagine what use I would be to a corporation. "Nestlé? What can I do for them?"

"We are trying to sell instant coffee in Japan, but we aren't having as much success as we would like. Your work on imprints might be very helpful to us."

We continued to talk and the man made me an extremely attractive offer. Not only were the financial terms considerable, but there was something promising about a project like this. Unlike my work with autistic children, where progress was painfully slow, this offer was a chance to quickly test theories I had developed about imprinting and the unconscious mind. It was an opportunity too good to pass up. I took a sabbatical and went off on my new assignment.

My first meeting with Nestlé executives and their Japanese advertising agency was very instructive. Their strategy, which today seems absurdly wrong but wasn't as obviously so in the 1970s, was to try to convince Japanese consumers to switch from tea to coffee. Having spent some time in Japan, I knew that tea meant a great deal to this culture, but I had no sense of what emotions they attached to coffee. I decided to gather several groups of people together to discover how they imprinted the beverage. I believed there was a message there that could open a door for Nestlé.

I structured a three-hour session with each of the groups. In the first hour, I took on the persona of a visitor from another planet, someone who had never seen coffee before and had no idea how one "used" it. I asked for help understanding the product, believing their descriptions would give me insight into what they thought of it.

In the next hour, I had them sit on the floor like elementary school children and use scissors and a pile of magazines to make a collage of words about coffee. The goal here was to get them to tell me stories with these words that would offer me further clues.

In the third hour, I had participants lie on the floor with pillows. There was some hesitation among members of every group, but I convinced them I wasn't entirely out of my mind. I put on soothing music and asked the participants to relax. What I was doing was calming their active brainwaves, getting them to that tranquil point just before sleep. When they reached this state, I took them on a journey back from their adulthood, past their teenage years, to a time when they were very young. Once they arrived, I asked them to think again about coffee and to recall their earliest memory of it, the first time they consciously experienced it, and their most significant memory of it (if that memory was a different one).

I designed this process to bring participants back to their first imprint of coffee and the emotion attached to it. In most cases, though, the journey led nowhere. What this signified for Nestlé was very clear. While the Japanese had an extremely strong emotional connection to tea (something I learned without asking in the first hour of the sessions), they had, at the most, a very superficial imprint of coffee. Most, in fact, had no imprint of coffee at all.

Under these circumstances, Nestlé's strategy of getting these consumers to switch from tea to coffee could only fail. Coffee could not compete with tea in the Japanese culture if it had such weak emotional resonance. Instead, if Nestlé was going to have any success in this market at all, they needed to start at the beginning. They needed to give the product meaning in this culture. They needed to create an imprint for coffee for the Japanese.

Armed with this information, Nestlé devised a new strategy. Rather than selling instant coffee to a country dedicated to tea, they created desserts for children infused with the flavor of coffee but without the caffeine. The younger generation embraced these desserts. Their first imprint of coffee was a very positive one, one they would carry throughout their lives. Through this, Nestlé gained a meaningful foothold in the Japanese market. While no marketer will likely ever be able to convince the Japanese to abandon tea, coffee sales—nearly nonexistent in 1970—now approach half a billion pounds per year in Japan. Understanding the process of imprinting—and how it related directly to Nestlé's marketing efforts—unlocked a door to the Japanese culture for them and turned around a floundering business venture.

It did something much more important for me, however. The realization that there was no significant imprint for coffee in Japan underscored for me that early imprinting has a tremendous impact on why people do what they do. In addition, the fact that the Japanese did not have a strong imprint for coffee while the Swiss (Nestlé is a Swiss company) obviously did made it clear that imprints vary from culture to culture. If I could get to the source of these imprints—if I could somehow "decode" elements of culture to discover the emotions and meanings attached to them—I would learn a great deal about human behavior and how it varies across the planet. This set me on the course of my life's work. I went off in search of the Codes hidden within the unconscious of every culture.

When a man and a woman have a child, they have a little human being rather than a bird, a fish, or an alligator. Their genetic code dictates this. When an American man and an American woman have a child, they have a little American. The reason for this is not genetic; it is because a different code—the Culture Code—is at work.

For example, "the sun" in French is *le soleil,* a masculine noun, and, for the French, a word closely associated with the Sun King, Louis XIV. The French, who imprint this reference at a young age, perceive the sun as male and, by extension, see males as brilliant and shining. Women, on the other hand, are associated with the moon, *la lune,* a feminine word. The moon, of course, does not shine by herself; she reflects the light of the sun. We can learn much about the relationship between French men and French women through this observation and the understanding of how French children receive the imprint of these terms.

For Germans, however, these words have nearly opposite meanings. The sun, *die Sonne,* is feminine, and Germans believe that women are the ones who bring warmth to the world, make things grow, and raise children. German men are the night, the dark, the moon side. *Der Mond,* "the moon," is a masculine term. Again, this speaks volumes about the relationships the genders have to each other in this culture and the roles they play in this society.

The simple acquisition of words like "sun" and "moon" can trigger completely opposite imprints among the French and Germans. Therefore, each culture has a different interpretation—a different Code—for these words. All of the different codes for all of the different imprints, when put together, create a reference system that people living in these cultures use without being aware of it. These reference systems guide different cultures in very different ways.

An imprint and its Code are like a lock and its combination. If you have all of the right numbers in the right sequence, you can open the lock. Doing so over a vast array of imprints has profound implications. It brings us to the answer to one of our most fundamental questions: why do we act the way we do? Understanding the Culture Code provides us with a remarkable new tool—a new set of glasses, if you will, with which to view ourselves and our behaviors. It changes the way we see everything around us. What's more, it confirms what we have always suspected is true—that, despite our common humanity, people around the world really *are* different. The Culture Code offers a way to understand how.

This book is the culmination of more than three decades of experience decoding imprints for major corporations around the world. I call this decoding process a "discovery"—I have performed more than three hundred—and I have seen these discoveries put to work to my clients' advantage. More than half of today's Fortune 100 companies have me on retainer, and corporate response to my findings has validated the accuracy of my work, assuring me that the glasses I have fashioned, the glasses of the Culture Code, offer a new and especially vivid vision of the world around us. Over the last thirty years, I have devised and patented a proven, tested method for making discoveries. In this book, I will share this method, and some of what I have learned about major world cultures by using it.

My primary intent is to liberate those who read this book. There is remarkable freedom gained in understanding why you act the way you do. This freedom will affect every part of your life, from the relationships you have, to your feelings about your possessions and the things you do, to the attitudes you have about America's place in the world.

The topics I will discuss in *The Culture Code* include many of the most significant forces driving our lives: sex, money, relationships, food, fat, health, and even America itself. You will see how participants in the discovery sessions led me to the Codes and how the revelation of the Codes led me to a new understanding of behavior in this country, how it contrasts with behavior in other cultures, and what these differences mean for all of us.

Once you know the Codes, nothing will ever look the same again.

Chapter 1

THE BIRTH OF A NOTION

I still run discovery sessions the same way I ran that first session for Nestlé more than thirty years ago. Five principles guide my methodology for uncovering cultural Codes, and knowledge of these principles will help you understand the thinking that goes into each discovery.

The best way to illustrate these principles is to look at them in the context of an actual discovery. In the following pages, I'll take you through the discovery of the American Code for cars. I did this several years ago for Chrysler, after the work I did for them on the Jeep Wrangler. They were preparing to launch a new vehicle and hired me to learn what people really wanted from cars. At the time, sales of sedans were flagging as Americans became more and more fascinated with SUVs, minivans, and trucks. Quite a few people in the industry even suggested that the public was no longer particularly interested in sedans at all. This discovery session was therefore critical to Chrysler in a number of ways, because if they learned that sedans no longer had appeal among Americans, it would dramatically alter the direction of the company.

PRINCIPLE 1: YOU CAN'T BELIEVE WHAT PEOPLE SAY

What do Americans look for in a car? I've heard many answers when I've asked this question. The answers include excellent safety ratings, great gas mileage, handling, and cornering ability, among others. I don't believe any of these. That's because the first principle of the Culture Code is that the only effective way to understand what people truly mean is to ignore what they say. This is not to suggest that people intentionally lie or misrepresent themselves. What it means is that, when asked direct questions about their interests and preferences, people tend to give answers they believe the questioner wants to hear. Again, this is not because they intend to mislead. It is because people respond to these questions with their cortexes, the parts of their brains that control intelligence rather than emotion or instinct. They ponder a question, they process a question, and when they deliver an answer, it is the product of deliberation. They believe they are telling the truth. A lie detector would confirm this. In most cases, however, they aren't saying what they mean.

The reason for this is simple: most people don't know why they do the things they do. In a classic study, the nineteenth-century scientist Jean-Martin Charcot hypnotized a female patient, handed her an umbrella, and asked her to open it. After this, he slowly brought the woman out of her hypnotic state. When she came to, she was surprised by the object she held in her hand. Charcot then asked her why she was carrying an open umbrella indoors. The woman was utterly confused by the question. She of course had no idea of what she had just been through and no memories of Charcot's instructions. Baffled, she looked at the ceiling. Then she looked back at Charcot and said, "It was raining."

Surely the woman didn't think she had an open umbrella indoors because it was raining. When asked, though, she felt the need to come up with an answer, and this was the only logical one she could devise.

Even the most self-examining of us are rarely in close contact with our subconscious. We have little interaction with this powerful force that drives so many of our actions. Therefore, we give answers to questions that sound logical and are even what the questioner expected, but which don't reveal the unconscious forces that precondition our feelings. This is why polls and surveys are so often misleading and useless (and why the executives at Chrysler got the wrong "answers" regarding the Wrangler). They simply reflect what people say, rather than what they mean.

Early in my career I realized that, if I wanted to help people identify what something really meant to them, I needed to adopt the role of "professional stranger," that visitor from another planet I wrote about earlier. I needed to convince people that I was a complete outsider who required their help in understanding how a particular item worked, what its appeal might be, or what emotions it was likely to provoke. What do you do with coffee? Is money some kind of clothing? How does one operate love? This allows people to begin the process of separating from their cortexes and moving toward the source of their first encounter with the item in question.

By the third hour of a discovery session—the point when the participants lie on the floor with pillows and listen to soothing music—people finally begin to say what they really mean. This process helps them access a different part of their brains. The answers they give now come from their reptilian brains, the place where their instincts are housed. It is in our reptilian brains that the real answers lie.

Many people have the experience of remembering their dreams vividly for the first five or ten minutes after they awaken. If they don't record the details of these dreams in those first few minutes, though, they usually lose them forever. This is because, during this state between sleep and wakefulness, you have better access to your memories and instincts. The relaxation process employed during the discovery sessions allows participants to access this state and in so doing to bypass their cortexes to reconnect with their reptilian brains. People regularly report that memories come back to them during these sessions that they had forgotten for years.

For Chrysler, I gathered participants and asked them to tell me what they wanted from a car. The initial responses I got were pure cortex: good gas mileage, safety, mechanical reliability, and all the other things we have learned to say about this subject. I, of course, did not believe them. As each session continued, I began to hear other things about cars that resonated. Memories of distinctive cars of the past, like the 1964½ Mustang, the original VW Beetle, and the Cadillacs of the 1950s with their huge fins. Stories of the sense of freedom that came with holding their first set of car keys. Bashful mutterings about first sexual experiences taking place in the back-seat of a car. Slowly, the sense of what American consumers really wanted from an automobile began to emerge. They wanted something distinctive. They wanted freedom. They wanted a sensual experience.

The car that emerged from these discovery sessions was the PT Cruiser, a car with a very strong look and a very strong message.

The reaction to the car was equally strong. Some people, of course, hated it. Any truly distinctive thing will be utterly unappealing to some people, even people within the same culture. This is because of the tensions that define cultures, something I will address at length in chapter 3.

However, others loved the car, so much that it became a big commercial success. Its release was the most successful new car launch in recent memory. People spent up to $4,000 extra just to be on a waiting list to own one. Did the groundswell of excitement come because the PT Cruiser provided what people said they wanted in a car? No. It had gas mileage and safety ratings no better than any number of sedans, and it was no more reliable mechanically. It was, however, unusual, aggressive, and sexy. It appealed to what people really wanted in a car rather than what they said they wanted. If we had listened only to what people said, Chrysler would have created another boring, efficient sedan and the public would have shrugged.

By learning what they really meant, Chrysler created a phenomenon instead.

PRINCIPLE 2: EMOTION IS THE ENERGY REQUIRED
TO LEARN ANYTHING

The discovery sessions for cars brought up some very strong emotions. People came to me after the third hour to say that memories brought them to tears, filled them with joy, or even made them extremely uncomfortable. This is not unusual. In fact, some form of this happens at nearly every discovery session I do—even the ones for office products and toilet paper.

Emotions are the keys to learning, the keys to imprinting. The stronger the emotion, the more clearly the experience is learned. Think again of that child and the hot pan. Emotions create a series of mental connections (I call them mental highways) that are reinforced by repetition. These mental highways condition us to see the world in predictable ways. They are the path from our experience with the world (such as touching a hot pan) to a useful approach to the world (avoiding all hot things in the future).

We do the overwhelming majority of our learning when we are children. By the time we are seven, most of our mental highways have been constructed. But emotion continues to provide us with new imprints throughout our lives. Most Americans of the Boomer generation can remember where they were and what they were doing when they learned of the assassination of John F. Kennedy. Most Americans alive today can vividly relive the experience of watching the World Trade Center towers fall. This is because these experiences are so emotionally powerful that they are effectively seared onto our brains. We will never forget them, and the simple mention of the topic sends us back to that moment when we imprinted it.

In Normandy, peasants have a strange and unpleasant ritual that exhibits an innate understanding of this concept at the same time that it shows a misguided approach to utilizing it. When the first son in a family reaches his seventh birthday, his father takes him out to the land the father owns and walks him to each corner of the property. At each corner, the father beats the child. While the practice is repellent and probably doesn't do much for the father-son bond, it does create a very strong emotional connection for the child to the boundaries of the property. The father knows that having this experience will cause the child to remember forever the bounds of the land he will some-day inherit.

I had my own unforgettable experience with learning an American phrase when I began teaching at Thomas Jefferson College not long after I arrived in this country in the seventies. I had only begun to learn how to speak American English. My class took place in a large, windowless lecture hall, and on the first day, I'd just started to explain my goals for the class when one of the students yelled at me, "Watch out!" I'd never heard the phrase before and therefore had no idea what the student meant. Instantly, my brain searched for some kind of definition. "Watch" meant "look." "Out" could mean "outside." Did the student want me to look outside? I couldn't, though, because there were no windows in the room. Of course, all of this happened in a fraction of a second—after which a part of the ceiling fell on my head and I was suddenly lying on the floor bleeding and waiting for paramedics to arrive.

To say the least, I now know what "watch out" means. In fact, whenever I hear it, I still look toward the ceiling first, just in case it's about to fall on me.

In our discovery session for cars that led to the PT Cruiser, it be-came clear that the emotions associated with the experience of driv-ing a car were very strong indeed. When people spoke about the moment when they were allowed to drive for the first time, they made it sound as though their lives began right then. Conversely, when elderly people spoke of the moment their car keys were taken away, they reported feeling as though their lives were over. Those first sexual experiences that for so many Americans take place in the backseat of a car (more than 80 percent of Americans have sex for the first time this way) send an incredibly strong emotional message about cars.

It became obvious to me that because the emotion associated with driving and owning a car is so strong, the PT Cruiser needed to be a car people could feel strongly about. It needed to have a distinctive identity to justify such strong emotions. To create a strong identity and a new car at the same time, we decided to tap into something that already existed in the culture, a familiar unconscious structure. The one we chose was the gangster car, the kind of vehicle Al Capone famously drove. This became the PT Cruiser's signature. It lent the car an extremely strong identity—there is nothing else like it on the road today—and the consumer responded. Again, if the Cruiser had been just another sedan, the public probably wouldn't have even noticed it, but its distinctiveness tapped into something very emotional.

PRINCIPLE 3: THE STRUCTURE, NOT THE CONTENT, IS THE MESSAGE

Unlike the sessions I did for the Jeep Wrangler, this new discovery had to do with cars in general. Predictably, participants spoke about all kinds of cars—minivans and roadsters, Model Ts and concept vehicles. How could I come to any conclusions about the Code when participants had such a wide range of cars in mind? By looking at the structure rather than the content.

In the play *Cyrano de Bergerac,* by Edmond Rostand, Cyrano has a dramatic swordfight. The Cyrano story was retold in the 1987 movie *Roxanne,* starring Steve Martin. Martin's character, C. D. Bales, has a similar encounter, but he uses a tennis racket. When one is looking for unconscious messages, the difference between swords and tennis rackets is irrelevant. They are merely the content. One can tell the same story with either a sword or a tennis racket, which means that the content isn't essential to the meaning. You could say the same thing about *West Side Story,* whose "content" is different from *Romeo and Juliet*'s but which tells the same tale.

What is important is the story's structure, the connection between the different elements. For both Cyrano and C. D., the fight is about defending honor. The need that leads to the fight is the important thing to identify, and it is the same in the two stories, even with different trappings.

One can say the same thing about a melody. You can play the same melody in the morning or the evening, on a piano or a violin, in the summer or the winter. The performers may be young or old, rich or poor, male or female. Even the notes are largely irrelevant, because a melody played in a different key or at a different octave is still the same melody. All of the aforementioned elements are the content. The structure is the space between the notes, the range between each note and its successor, and the rhythm.

The key to understanding the true meanings behind our actions is to understand the structure. The anthropologist Claude Lévi-Strauss studied kinship, saying that he was not interested in people but in the relationships between them, the "space between the people." An uncle does not exist if there is no niece, a wife if there is no husband, a mother if there is no child. Kinship is the structure.

When looking at why people act in certain ways or do certain things, we need to look past the content and into the structure. In any situation, there are three distinct structures in action. The first is the biological structure, the DNA. Monkeys, human beings, cows, and giraffes are made of the same content. However, each species is unique because the organization of its DNA—its structure—is unique.

The next structure is the culture. All cultures have a language, an art, a habitat, a history, and so on; the way all these elements, this content, is organized creates the unique identity of each culture.

The final structure is the individual. Within the DNA that makes us human there is an infinite variety. Further, each of us has a unique relationship with our parents, siblings, and family that shapes our individual mental scripts and creates our unique identity. Even identical twins end up with unique identities. One was born first, the other second. They are never going to be at exactly the same place at the same time, and, little by little, they will start developing different perspectives on the world. They begin with the same content but develop different structures.

When I read the third-hour stories participants tell in discovery sessions, I pay no attention to the content; instead, I focus exclusively on the structure. In the sessions I held for Chrysler, it was irrelevant that one participant told a story about a sports car while another talked about the family sedan and yet another yearned for his 1950 Packard. It didn't matter if they took their cars into the city, down country lanes, or out on the open highway. What mattered was the connection between the driver and the car, between the experience of driving and the feelings evoked. These connections—this structure— gave us the clear sense that Americans derive a strong sense of identity from their cars, and led to the development of a car that would reinforce that sense of identity.

PRINCIPLE 4: THERE IS A WINDOW IN TIME FOR IMPRINTING, AND THE MEANING OF THE IMPRINT VARIES FROM ONE CULTURE TO ANOTHER

I like to say that you never get a second chance to have a first experience. Most of us imprint the meanings of the things most central to our lives by the age of seven. This is because emotion is the central force for children under the age of seven (if you need proof of this, watch how often a young child's emotional state changes in a single hour), while after this, they are guided by logic (again, try arguing with a nine-year-old). Most people are exposed to only one culture before the age of seven. They spend most of this time at home or within their local environment. Few young Americans are exposed in any meaningful way to Japanese culture. Few Japanese children are exposed to Irish culture. Therefore, the extremely strong imprints placed in their subconscious at this early age are determined by the culture in which they are raised. An American child's most active period of learning happens in an American context. Mental structures formed in an American environment fill his subconscious. The child therefore grows up an American.

This is why people from different cultures have such different reactions to the same things. Let's take, for example, peanut butter. Americans receive a strong emotional imprint from peanut butter. Your mother makes you a peanut-butter-and-jelly sandwich when you are little, and you associate it with her love and nurturance. Since I was born in France, where peanut butter is not a household staple, I never made this connection. I learned about peanut butter after the closing of the window in time when I could form a strong emotional association with it. Because it didn't carry with it the weight of my mother's love, it was simply another foodstuff. I tasted it and didn't find it to be special in any way; in fact, I didn't like it. Cheese, however, which has a prominent place in every French household, is another matter entirely. I can't possibly taste cheese without my subconscious layering that taste with emotional connections from my youth.

My teenage son, Dorian, is very much an American in most ways, but because he has always spent time with me in the house I keep in France, he has learned about certain things the way a French child learns about them. One example is champagne. In France, people drink champagne, as they do all wine, for its taste, not its alcohol content. The purpose of drinking wine in France is almost never to get drunk, but to enjoy the flavor of the wine and the way it enhances food.

French children get their first taste of champagne at a very early age. They dip sugar cubes or cookies into it and in doing so learn its flavor and distinctive qualities. Dorian would often have a taste of champagne with us in France; thus he learned to appreciate it and to associate it with celebration, since in France, we most often drink champagne when we are celebrating something. One time, a group of us went to an American restaurant for a celebration and ordered champagne. Dorian, who was seven or eight at the time, asked for a glass, and the waiter scoffed. When I told the waiter it was okay, he still didn't believe me (or perhaps he felt legally bound to ignore me). He mixed a concoction of club soda and a dash of orange juice in a champagne glass and handed it to Dorian—who tasted it and immediately rejected it because he was well aware of the flavor of champagne.

Most Americans receive their first real imprint of alcohol when they are teenagers. This is a very different window in time from the one in which the French learn about alcohol, and therefore the connection made is different. For most Americans, alcohol serves a function: it makes you drunk. Few American teens ponder the bouquet of the beer they guzzle. Several of Dorian's friends have already had problems with drunkenness because they associate alcohol with inebriation rather than with taste. They have learned that alcohol can do a job for them, and nothing more. Many of them, in fact, respond to alcohol the way I responded to peanut butter—they find the taste unappealing—but they forge ahead because they know doing so will change their state of mind.

To return to our PT Cruiser session again, I learned that cars are an essential part of American culture because, while American children don't experience the emotion of driving a car at an early age, they imprint the thrills associated with cars in their youth. Americans love cars and they love going out in them. Throughout the discovery sessions, participants told stories of their excited parents bringing home a new car, about the enjoyment and bonding that comes from families going out for drives together on the weekend, about the breathtaking first ride in a sports car. American children learn at an early age that cars are an essential and vaunted part of family life, that they bring joy and even family unity. When it is time for them to buy a car, this emotional connection guides them subconsciously. They want a car that feels special to them. The distinctiveness of the PT Cruiser gave them this feeling, so they welcomed it into their garages and their lives.

PRINCIPLE 5: TO ACCESS THE MEANING OF AN IMPRINT WITHIN A PARTICULAR CULTURE, YOU MUST LEARN THE CODE FOR THAT IMPRINT

The PT Cruiser was a smash success in America. Yet prior to its release, the new executives at DaimlerChrysler predicted it would fail. Why? Because different cultures have different Codes.

Even our most arbitrary actions are the result of the trips we take down our mental highways. We take these trips hundreds of times a day, making decisions about what to wear, what to eat, where to go, what to say in conversation, and so on. What most people don't realize, however, is that there is a Code required to make these journeys. Think of the Code as a combination that unlocks a door. In this case, we need not only to punch in the numbers, but also to punch them in in a specific order, at a specific speed, with a specific rhythm, etc. Every word, every action, and every symbol has a Code. Our brains supply these Codes subconsciously, but there is a way to discover them, to understand why we do the things we do.

As I've already illustrated, the discovery sessions I conduct for my clients allow us to learn what a particular thing really means to our participants. When my staff and I analyze participant responses after a session, common messages emerge. We discover the Codes when we find these common messages.

These messages vary greatly from culture to culture, and, therefore, so do the Codes. For example, I conducted discovery sessions about cheese in France and in America. The Codes we uncovered could not have been more different. The French Code for cheese is ALIVE. This makes perfect sense when one considers how the French choose and store cheese. They go to a cheese shop and poke and prod the cheeses, smelling them to learn their ages. When they choose one, they take it home and store it at room temperature in a cloche (a bell-shaped cover with little holes to allow air in and keep insects out). The American Code for cheese, on the other hand, is DEAD. Again, this makes sense in context. Americans "kill" their cheese through pasteurization (unpasteurized cheeses are not allowed into this country), select hunks of cheese that have been prewrapped—mummified, if you will—in plastic (like body bags), and store it, still wrapped airtight, in a morgue also known as a refrigerator.

There is a movement in Europe (instigated by some bureaucrats in Brussels) to impose pasteurization laws throughout the European Union. Knowing what you now know about the French Code for cheese and what pasteurization does to cheese, have you any doubt how the French have reacted to this movement? Their response was so intense that there were even demonstrations in the streets. The notion of forcing the French to pasteurize their cheese is decidedly "off Code."

This perspective really holds for foods of all kinds. Americans are intensely concerned with food safety. We have regulatory commissions, expiration dates, and a wide variety of "food police" out there protecting us from unsafe food. The French, on the other hand, are far more interested in taste than safety. In France, there is a method of preparation known as *faisandée*. It involves hanging a pheasant (the source of the name) or some other gamebird on a hook until it ages— literally, until it begins to rot. While most Americans would consider the thought of this alarming, French chefs utilize this method because it dramatically improves the flavor of the bird. Safety is not nearly as much of a concern for them or the people for whom they cook. Of course, such culinary explorations come with a price. There are far more food-related deaths in France every year than there are in the United States, even though there are five times as many people living in the United States.

We can return one more time to our example of the PT Cruiser to show how these different cultural Codes affect our responses to things. My review of hundreds of stories told by participants during the discovery sessions revealed that the American Code for cars is IDENTITY. Americans want cars that are distinctive, that will not be mistaken for any other kind of car on the road, and that trigger memories of Sunday drives, the freedom of getting behind the wheel for the first time, and the excitement of youthful passion. A car with a strong identity, such as the PT Cruiser or, as I illustrated earlier, the Jeep Wrangler, has a much better chance of breakout sales than a cookie-cutter sedan.

This Code, however, is far from universal across cultures. German automotive giant Daimler-Benz purchased Chrysler around the time the PT Cruiser was on its way to production. When the German executives who now ran the company saw the car, they were appalled. Why? Because the Code for cars in the German culture is decidedly different from the American one. The German Code for cars is ENGINEERING. German car manufacturers pride themselves on the quality of their engineering, and this pride is so ingrained that people raised in that culture think of engineering first when they think of cars. The initial PT Cruisers were in no way models of engineering excellence. Their engines weren't particularly powerful or efficient, the design was anything but streamlined, they didn't handle very well, and their gas mileage and safety ratings were only average. The new executive team at Chrysler, accessing their cultural Code, believed the PT Cruiser would be a marketing disaster. They relegated production to one plant in Mexico.

This turned out to be a huge (although understandable) mistake. German executives responded negatively to the modest quality of the car's engineering. American consumers responded positively to the car's high level of identity. The plant in Mexico was ill equipped to keep up with demand, and there were long waiting lists. If the new executives at Chrysler had understood the American Code for cars, and had relied on it rather than on their own Code, they would have avoided the many problems they had getting the desired number of PT Cruisers onto American highways.

A NOTION IS BORN: DISCOVERING THE CULTURAL UNCONSCIOUS

The notion supported by these five principles is that there is a third unconscious at work. The principles cannot be ascribed to either the Freudian individual unconscious that guides each of us in unique ways or the Jungian collective unconscious that guides each of us as members of the human race. The principles illuminate an unconscious that uniquely guides each of us depending on the cultures that produced us. The third unconscious is the cultural unconscious.

This notion and these principles are irrefutable evidence that there is an American mind, just as there is a French mind, an English mind, a Kurdish mind, and a Latvian mind. Every culture has its own mind-set, and that mind-set teaches us about who we are in profound ways.

In the remainder of this book, I will lead you to the two dozen most important Codes I have discovered. These Codes will show how the cultural unconscious affects our personal lives, the decisions we make as consumers, and the way we operate as citizens of the world. I will also contrast these Codes with discoveries I have made in other cultures to show how the same thing can have very different meaning elsewhere. There are more than a few "wow" moments in this book. There are revelations here that will help you conduct yourself, do business, and regard others with new clarity.

Let's go fit you with a new set of glasses.

Chapter 2

THE GROWING PAINS OF AN
ADOLESCENT CULTURE

The Codes for Love, Seduction, and Sex

C ultures are created and evolve over time, though the rate of
change is glacial. A culture might not experience a significant shift for generations. When cultures *do* change, the
changes occur in the same way as in our brains—via powerful imprints. These powerful imprints alter the "reference system" of the
culture, and the significance is passed down to subsequent generations. Indians, for example, consider Hanuman langur monkeys sacred because a Hindu epic written more than twenty centuries ago
tells of one such monkey rescuing the king's abducted queen. The imprint of this legend is so strong within the culture that these monkeys
are still free to roam wherever they want in India, even though they
regularly stop traffic, invade grain storehouses, and prove a general
nuisance.

A culture-founding and culture-changing imprint of another variety took place in ancient Israel. There, neighboring pagan tribes offered pigs as a sacred sacrifice to their idols, a practice Jews found
repellent. Compounding this, pigs were filthy animals back then,
feeding on carrion and garbage. Eating pork caused the spread of terrible diseases and weakened the community. In response, the Jewish
religion forbade the consumption of pork, and many Jews still avoid

pork even though most have no contact with pagan rituals and pigs are raised under conditions in which their meat is unlikely to spread parasites. Again, the imprint of scores of villagers becoming deathly ill from meat-borne parasites or witnessing shocking rites was so strong that the culture shifted.

Imprints this strong happen infrequently. Therefore, cultures emerge and change slowly. At slightly more than two and a quarter centuries old, the American culture has experienced relatively few culture-changing imprints. The opening of the West, the waves of persecuted people coming to these shores and finding success, and our country's emerging as a protector in two world wars were such imprints. It is very possible that we experienced another culture-changing imprint on September 11, 2001, but we will only be certain of this a few generations from now. Regardless, if one were to equate life stages to the evolution of a culture, we are very young. Not as young as the Canadian culture or the South African culture, certainly, but decidedly younger than the elderly British or Japanese. We are, in fact, in the full throes of adolescence—and this metaphor extends beyond our relative age as a culture into the way we act and react.

IF YOU DON'T KILL THE KING, YOU CAN STAY YOUNG FOREVER

Our cultural adolescence informs our behavior in a wide variety of ways. It is an incredibly powerful part of our reference system, maybe the strongest in our culture. The theme of adolescence shows up in nearly every American discovery session. Conversely, themes associated with age—patience, sophistication, and the understanding of limits, among others—emerge with great regularity in discovery sessions held in older cultures. You'll see the contrast between adolescent themes and adult themes throughout this book.

Our adolescence stems from one essential point: we never had to kill the king in order to become who we are.

Every adult was once a child, small and anxious. Then they go through stages of adolescence and rebellion. In the American culture, however, our rebellion took an unusual form. Many cultures act out their rebellion by killing their leaders (for example, the French rebelled by beheading Louis XVI), after which their period of rebellion ends and adulthood begins. We never killed our king because we never actually had one. We rebelled against the only king who ever tried to rule us and threw him out of "our room," but we didn't behead him. We simply told him to stay out.

For this reason, our rebellious period never really ended. Rather than moving on from it, we hold on to it and reinforce it when we welcome immigrants to our shores. These immigrants have left the country that was forced upon them at birth. Coming here is a huge act of rebellion. Like the American revolutionaries, they leave their old cultures behind rather than "finishing the job" by killing the king. Therefore, they remain rebels, and this constant influx of new adolescents helps keep our entire culture adolescent.

Looking at our culture through this set of glasses explains why we are so successful around the world selling the trappings of adolescence: Coca-Cola, Nike shoes, fast food, blue jeans, and loud, violent movies. America has never produced a world-class classical composer, but has successfully exported rock, hip-hop, and R&B—the music of adolescence—to every corner of the globe. American basketball players who can hardly read make exponentially more money than American scientists do. We are endlessly fascinated with celebrities and all the adolescent mistakes they make.

THE WACKO CULTURE

For example, Americans love Mike Tyson, Michael Jackson, Tom Cruise, Venus Williams, and Bill Clinton. We love them for several reasons. Primarily, though, we love them because they are weird, eccentric, and nowhere near the middle. They show us that extreme behavior is perfectly acceptable. We love them because, like Jennifer Wilbanks (the Runaway Bride), they are afraid to grow up. In reality, they are nothing more than "Runaway Adults."

The New York Times recently wrote, "Mike Tyson maintains a magnetism that leaves sociologists struggling for explanations." *USA Today* says that Tyson is "flying . . . and then falling. Up and down, immobile and . . . in jail. Therapist says troubled Tyson has decided it's time to grow up."

Who wants to grow up, though?

A typical American expression is "I still don't know what I want to do when I grow up." You will hear it often from people in their sixties or seventies.

Michael Jackson does not want to face the reality of his age. Nearing fifty, he still wants to sleep with children. It is fine when you are nine or ten to sleep over at a friend's house. When you are forty-seven and sleeping with twelve-year-olds, though . . .

Oprah Winfrey invited Tom Cruise on her show to promote one of his movies. Instead, he spent the hour promoting "It's okay to be weird" behavior. During the show, he jumped around the set, hopped onto a couch, fell rapturously to one knee, and repeatedly professed his love for his new girlfriend. When my kids were nine, they used to jump on their beds for an hour. I never confused this with grown-up behavior, and people have responded to Cruise's "jumping on the bed" in a similar way. At the same time, though, right after his *Oprah* appearance, they bought $65 million worth of tickets to his new movie in its first weekend.

Venus Williams won the 2005 Wimbledon championship, the most stiff-upper-lip tennis tournament in the world. Her dress was sedate and white, but she could not repress her exuberant adolescent joy and started jumping in the air after her victory like a nine-year-old on a bed.

Bill Clinton was a political genius, not for his understanding of world problems, but for his ability to resonate with the American cultural unconscious. Clinton was the perfect adolescent president. Fantastic material for the stand-up comedian: cheating, lying under oath, a sex scandal—the whole package was perfect.

What these figures have in common and what fascinates us so much is their resistance to growing up. They are forever young at heart, crazy, up and down, one day invincible, one day totally rejected, and they always come back. They are the "eternal adolescents" all Americans would love to be.

At the same time, they are a victory for nonconformity. In America, you can be weird and successful. As the journalist Jack Miller wrote, "Creative artists and performers who are wildly eccentric, who do not look like the rest of us, who live in a reality unfathomable to the majority deserve praise, kindness and appreciation for their talents and their gift of genius. Vive la différence."

This is the "wacko" culture. Would you rather be part of an adolescent culture or a senile one?

THE AMERICAN CULTURE: ADOLESCENT THROUGH AND THROUGH

As you will learn throughout this book, the American culture exhibits many of the traits consistent with adolescence: intense focus on the "now," dramatic mood swings, a constant need for exploration and challenge to authority, a fascination with extremes, openness to change and reinvention, and a strong belief that mistakes warrant second chances. As Americans, we feel we know more than our elders do (for instance, we rarely consult France, Germany, Russia, or England on our foreign policy), that their answers are out of date (we pay little heed to the opinions of these cultures when it comes to global matters), and that we must reject their lessons and remake the world (few of us—even our leaders—are students of world history, choosing to make our own mistakes rather than learn from the mistakes other cultures have already made).

Like all adolescents, we are preoccupied with love, seduction, and sex. We are not unique in this regard. People in many cultures throughout the world are fascinated with these things, perhaps more than with anything else. After all, as human beings, we need sex at the very least to ensure the continuation of our species. The unconscious attitudes we Americans hold about these matters, however, are unique and are closely related to our cultural adolescence.

Adolescence is a time of confusion and contradictions. New discoveries are promising one day and disappointing the next. Dreams sprout, flower, and wilt as quickly as daffodils in the spring. Certainties become uncertainties in the blink of an eye. This is as true of adolescent cultures as it is of adolescent children, and nowhere is it clearer than in the Codes revealed in this chapter.

Some of you will find the following pages disturbing. Some of you will insist that you don't see yourself in these Codes in any way. (You might even be right about that. *Of course,* every individual is different, as he or she is also governed by his or her individual unconscious.) The revelation of the following Codes might be upsetting to you, but please remember that Codes are value neutral. The Codes themselves do not pass judgment on a particular culture. The American Codes simply reflect our cultural adolescence. This is very good and empowering in many cases, as you will see in subsequent chapters, and it explains why we are the best in the world at many things and why we have been such innovators and reformers.

If one were to compile a list of things at which the American culture excels, however, love, seduction, and sex would not be on that list. You know this already. After all, when we consider someone a great ladies' man, we might call him a "Don Juan" or a "Casanova." We will never, however, call him a "Joe Smith." The function of the new set of glasses provided by the Culture Code is to show us *why* we do the things we do:

Why are American women so concerned with finding "Mr. Right"?

Why does the FCC frown on (and even prosecute) the televising of a woman breast-feeding, but allow the exhibition of fictionalized bloodbaths during network prime time?

Why are American women offended when construction workers whistle at them in New York, but flattered when a man does the same in Milan?

The answers are in the Codes.

WHAT'S LOVE GOT TO DO WITH IT?

I held imprinting sessions all over the country, searching for the Code for love. During these sessions, I asked participants to focus on the word "love" without specifying whether I meant romantic love, parental love, sibling love, love of country, love of pets, or even love of a sports team. When I guided participants back to their first imprint, though, a vast majority of them went to the same place.

> My first experience with the word "love," or related to love, was when I was four or five. In the kitchen, Mother was preparing a cake, my favorite cake, a cheesecake. The smell was the smell of love. She opened the oven and I told her, "I love you!" She closed the oven, came to give me a kiss, and told me, "I love you, too." Then she gave me a big portion of the cake and I knew she really meant it when she said, "I love you."—*a forty-year-old man*

> Mother loved us so much, she cooked all Thanksgiving Day. She was so happy to see her family all together again, around the table, eating . . . so much love around the table, so much food. We could not stop eating.—*a thirty-six-year-old woman*

When you are little, parents are there to care for and protect you. You have no cares or worries. If something bad happens, your family is there for you. I miss this protection.—*a fifty-eight-year-old woman*

The best way to describe my parents' room is a nest. The carpet was light brown and the walls were blue. The bed was in the center of the room and had a huge white comforter. It was on this bed that I sat with my mother as a child and asked her about the world.—*a twenty-one-year-old man*

I remember lying in my mother's lap in my early years. I remember talking with my mother and sharing caresses.—*a sixty-five-year-old man*

Consistently, participants related their first experience of love to their mother's care—feeding them, holding them, making them feel safe. This is entirely understandable. After all, for nine months, our mothers provide us with the most perfect "resort hotel" imaginable. The room service is first-rate and available immediately upon demand, the space is neither too hot nor too cold, transportation is free, and there's even a musical backdrop (her heartbeat) for entertainment. And even though we ultimately must leave this vacation paradise, our mothers are there to guide us through the transition, feeding us with their bodies, keeping us coddled and warm, taking us out to see the world, and providing numerous ways for us to occupy our time and to delight in the act of learning.

These responses were very consistent with the thinking of an adolescent culture. Adolescents, after all, flit from pressing for independence to acting like children; in the latter mode, they seek the succor (inwardly, if not overtly) of their mothers, the safe harbor provided by that all-encompassing love.

Then there is the "independence" mode, the mode that demands a rejection of home and the right to make one's own mistakes. When I asked participants to recall their most powerful memories of love, different stories emerged.

> I went to college. I was so happy. Free at last. But it did not go so well. First time I started drinking, I could not stop. Then I don't know what happened next, I was so sick. None of the boys who were after me the night before were there to help me.
> —*a fifty-year-old woman*

> I was thirteen and I liked a boy but he liked someone else. This taught me a big lesson, because I thought that I was prettier than her and she was fat, but I was spoiled and sometimes mean.
> —*a twenty-four-year-old woman*

> My most powerful experience is when my parents decided to separate. I found out eavesdropping on their discussions late at night. Things were tense, but everyone wanted to be normal.
> —*a thirty-seven-year-old man*

> I have an image of a white beautiful horse and a blond beautiful woman in a flowing crepe-like dress with a lush green forest and waterfall and a handsome man meeting and embracing her. I long to be that woman.—*a thirty-eight-year-old woman*

This was a different component of the adolescent experience: the part where experimentation leads to exhilaration and disappointment, to success and failure. The vast majority of these stories expressed some degree of discomfort, of uneasiness with the events described, much as an adolescent describes experiences he doesn't like and doesn't understand. Remember, these stories were about the *most powerful* memory of love.

Perhaps the most significant element of the adolescent experience, however, is the loss of innocence. There comes a point in every adolescent's life when he realizes his ideals aren't as gilded as they once seemed. This realization usually leads to new maturity and the acquisition of new coping tools. It also often comes, though, with a sense of disillusionment. When participants wrote of their most recent memory of love, they repeatedly told the story of lost ideals.

> I know what boys want. They say they love you, but I know what they want.—*a thirty-five-year-old woman*

> I have three children from three different fathers who died in drive-by shootings. Before I die, I want once again to have a baby, to feed him, to love him, and to be loved unconditionally. —*a fifteen-year-old woman*

> I purchased a diamond for my girlfriend. I recall her taking it off in the car while we were arguing and I became infuriated. I took the ring and threw it out the window. I told her since it meant so little to her, I threw it away.—*a thirty-one-year-old man*

These three sets of stories—the first imprint, the most powerful memory, and the most recent memory—revealed a distinctly American pattern. Participants spoke repeatedly of the desire for love, the need for love, the belief in something called true love, but they also spoke consistently of being disappointed in this quest. A very large percentage of the "most recent memory" stories spoke of loss, bitterness, and sadness. Americans—regardless of their age—view love the way an adolescent views the world: as an exciting dream that rarely reaches fulfillment.

The American Culture Code for love is FALSE EXPECTATION.

Without question, losing at love is an international experience. Even in cultures where marriages are arranged and courtship is rare, there are tales of forbidden love and of the sad consequences when that love dies. In older cultures, though—ones that passed through adolescence centuries ago—the unconscious message about the expectations for love are very different.

In France, the concepts of love and pleasure are intertwined. The French consider the notions of true love and Mr. Right irrelevant. The refinement of pleasure is paramount, and romance is a highly sophisticated process. Love means helping your partner achieve as much pleasure as possible, even if this requires finding someone else to provide some of this pleasure. French couples can, of course, be devoted to each other, but their definition of devotion differs greatly from the American definition (fidelity, for instance, is not nearly as important to them), and their expectations are set accordingly.

The Italians believe that life is a comedy rather than a tragedy and that one should laugh whenever possible. They expect love to contain strong dimensions of pleasure, beauty, and, above all, fun. If love becomes too dramatic or too hard, it is unsatisfying. The Italian culture centers very strongly on family, and Italians put their mothers up on pedestals. To them, true love is maternal love. Therefore, their expectations for romantic love are lower. Men romance women, but seek true love from their mothers. Women believe that the best way to express and experience love is by becoming mothers. A man is Mr. Right as long as he provides a child.

The Japanese offer perhaps the best illustration of the differences in attitudes toward love between an adolescent culture and an older culture. Japanese men and women often ask me to describe how Westerners marry. I tell them that a young man meets a young woman (often one younger than he) and they begin the process of getting to know each other. If he happens to fall deeply in love, the man will ask the woman to marry him, and if she loves him as well, she will say yes. (Obviously, it's more complicated that this in practice, but I get the main points across this way.)

Stunned expressions always meet this description. "The man is young?" the Japanese questioner will say. "If he is young, how can he possibly have enough experience to make a decision of this type? Only his parents can know what kind of marriage is appropriate for him and will allow him to raise the best family. And you say the woman is younger. That means she is even less experienced than he is!"

They save their greatest contempt, though, for the notion that Westerners marry for love. "Love is a *temporary disease,*" they tell me. "It is foolish to base something as important as the creation of a family on something so temporary." This is still the prevalent sensibility in Japan today, even though the "content" of Japanese culture has changed. While Japanese teens might date more often than their parents did, and might spend more time meeting up at clubs, most marriages are still arranged and few have anything to do with romance. This all might sound terribly harsh to American ears, but there is at least some logic in it: while nearly half of all American marriages end in divorce, the Japanese divorce rate is less than 2 percent.

This is not to suggest that older cultures necessarily have a clearer vision of the world. In fact, as you will see over the course of this book, there are many instances where the "adolescent" approach is the more effective one. When it comes to love, however, it is obvious that the American culture is currently in an uneasy place. A woman searches for Mr. Right because she believes the stories she reads in books or watches at the movies; she finds someone she believes she can "change" into her ideal man, and she disappointedly sees her efforts fail. A man searches for Ms. Perfect for many of the same reasons; he finds a woman who excites him, he believes it will stay this way forever, and he is disappointed when motherhood takes her interests elsewhere.

This quest for perfection is, of course, on Code: our cultural unconscious compels us to have unrealistically high standards for love. However, as that 50 percent divorce rate indicates, the Code isn't making our lives easier. Here is a case where an understanding of the Code can help those frustrated by love to go off Code in a productive manner. If you realize that your unconscious *expects* you to fail, you can begin to look at love with more sensible goals. While understanding and respecting the tug to find Mr. Right or Ms. Perfect, you can look for someone who can be a partner, a friend, and a caring lover, though she or he can't possibly fulfill all of your needs.

A prominent diamond company deals with the Code in a distinctive fashion. One component of its marketing focuses on the "false expectations" the American subconscious feels about love. its ads feature couples using diamonds to profess their eternal love or to confirm their commitment after years together. Another component of its marketing, however, deals with the consequences of false expectations in a clever manner: by highlighting the investment and resale value of diamonds. Both campaigns are strongly on Code, addressing our undying belief in the permanence of romantic love and providing a useful benefit when that belief fails to pan out.

WHY DOES SEDUCTION MAKE US DANGEROUSLY UNCOMFORTABLE?

I was eleven years old. I was shopping with my mother. I already had a figure, a nice bust, but my mother didn't want me to wear makeup. A middle-aged man was looking at me and came up to speak to me. My mom was right there like Superman saying, "You dirty old man." She took my hand and we moved to another aisle. At first, I did not understand what happened. I just got a feeling of danger.—*a fifty-six-year-old American woman, on her first imprint of seduction*

When the French beauty product company L'Oréal commissioned me to perform imprinting sessions on seduction all over the world, I got the opportunity to juxtapose the American Culture Code for this against the Codes of cultures that had long since passed beyond adolescence. It wasn't at all surprising that the American Code was different from those of the older cultures. However, from the very first session I held in the United States, I found that responses were consistent, in a way both revealing and, indeed, surprising. Something about the very notion of seduction makes us Americans squeamish.

I was in kindergarten. This little boy was very nice with me, always telling me he liked me and always playing with my toys. One day, he left with one of my stuffed animals. I saw it, but did not cry or say anything because I wanted him to come back and play with me.—*a fifty-one-year-old woman*

These responses were unlike any I received anywhere else in the world. Of course, each culture has its own distinct impressions of seduction and the seduction ritual. The French, for instance, have a popular saying: "It's not what you have; it's what you do with it." Unlike American women, who try to change what nature gave them through plastic surgery, liposuction, whitened and capped teeth, and endless hours at the gym, French women seek to enhance their natural appearance. In France, a woman will spend two hours in front of the mirror trying to appear as though she hasn't spent any time on her makeup at all. Her goal is to seem as casual about her seductive qualities as possible. In fact, if a French woman appears obviously made up, there's a good chance she'll be mistaken for a prostitute.

Showing that you are trying too hard to get a man indicates that you are desperate, and this is frowned upon in French culture. This even extends to the names of attire chosen as part of seduction. The word "negligee" comes from a French root that roughly translates in English to "neglect." Even though a French woman might look especially appealing in a negligee, her intent is to appear as though she doesn't care at all about what she's wearing.

The concept of makeup and preparation for seduction came up very infrequently in the American imprinting sessions. When it did, it was usually associated with a parent's scorn.

> My first experience with seduction was when I was a little girl. I
> was stealing my mother's makeup and lipstick and with two of
> my friends, we would pretend we were grown up—wearing my
> mother's high heels, walking slowly, trying to be models on a cat-
> walk. My mother would arrive and be upset because we ruined
> her makeup.—*a fifty-five-year-old woman*

The English, on the other hand, perform the seduction dance to much louder music, and only one gender seems to be doing any dancing at all.

English men have a remarkably strong bond with one another, perhaps stronger than the relationship between men in any other culture. Because they truly believe that only other men can understand their feelings, all of their meaningful friendships are with other men. They spend a great deal of time in men's clubs, and most of their nights out center around activities with other men, even if they wind up going home with a woman when the evening is over.

This understandably leads to a real disconnection from English women, who feel left out of the party. The lack of attention they receive from the men of their culture is extremely frustrating and distressing to them. Because they feel unnoticed and unacknowledged, young English women prepare for seduction in a way almost precisely the opposite of French women. They dress outrageously to gain attention. They'll wear miniskirts barely bigger than a belt, they'll expose their midriffs and adorn their navels with jewelry, and they'll dye their hair a variety of colors, often at the same time. They make every effort to be noticed.

Yet English men tend to remain detached. Detachment is, in fact, a signature of the English man (think of the scene in the movie *Titanic* where, while others run for safety from the sinking ship, an Englishman continues to play cards, saying, "I have a good hand; I'd like to finish it out"). It is a rare occasion indeed when you see an English man walk down the street, see a beautiful woman, and comment in any way.

This simply causes English women to ratchet up their efforts. Given the direction in which this is heading, one can only imagine what the fashion trends will be in London a couple of decades from now.

American women are rarely this provocative. Again, this is a reflection of our cultural adolescence, a stage known for awkwardness and uncertainty. In America, there is an undercurrent of fear of the ramifications of overtly sexual behavior, exemplified by this response from a participant in an imprinting session:

When I was in high school, I saw two guys trying to catch a girl. They were playing, but suddenly the fight became ugly. One guy touched the girl's breast and she punched him in the nose. The teacher arrived. The girl said the guys were trying to rape her. That was a mess. Since then, I did not want to play this kind of game with boys.—*a twenty-five-year-old woman*

The Italian culture, an ancient one, sends very different unconscious messages to those raised within it. Italians see seduction as an elaborate and joyous game. Italian men adore women and embrace everything about them. They are more in touch with their feminine side than men of any other culture are (remember, when we speak about a Culture Code, we aren't saying everyone is alike, but that this reference system is available to everyone in the culture). In fact, they spend more time beautifying themselves than Italian women do. They make liberal use of cosmetics, use baby shampoo to make their hair soft and lustrous, apply creams and ointments to their skin to keep their appearance youthful, and take tremendous care in the way they dress—their clothes, their shoes, and their fragrance. They are probably the most elegant men in the world, and the objective of this elegance is seduction.

Because they have such a strong feminine side, Italian men connect very easily with women; Italian women love them for it. In fact, even foreign women respond differently to Italian men than they do to men of other cultures. While in their home country, women might be offended if men whistled at them (think of an American woman passing construction workers), they are often charmed if the same thing happens on an Italian street. Largely, this is because Italian men make it clear that their attentions are in fun and neither threatening nor salacious in any way; their strong natural connection to women makes it easy for them to convey this.

In fact, seduction is more of a pastime for Italian men than it is for people of either gender in any other culture. It is a game in which playing is much more important than winning. An Italian man will go up to a woman he doesn't know, he'll tell her how beautiful she is and that he has fallen in love with her instantly—and, if the woman doesn't reciprocate his interest, he'll merely smile, shrug, and move along. Five minutes later, you can find him doing the same thing with another woman and, if the results are the same, he'll keep going until he encounters someone who considers him irresistible. Remarkably, he actually stands a decent chance of succeeding with this approach.

I got little sense of this playful side from American men in the discovery sessions I held. To the contrary, male American participants consistently wrote about the adolescent emotions of confusion, disappointment, and desperation.

> I have never been good at that. I was very uncomfortable with girls. They were always laughing and I did not know why. I felt ashamed, but I did not know why.—*a twenty-year-old man*

> When I was a child (four or five), people told me I was cute. I had a girlfriend my age in school. We were always together, sometimes holding hands. The teacher told our respective parents and I was not allowed to be with her anymore. I think she was my first love. I was so sad, I cried for days.—*a thirty-five-year-old man*

> I had principles. My friends were laughing and telling me I would never get laid, I was too ugly. My friends always spoke about sex in high school. I was not comfortable with them. I wanted to find a girl who would love me. I was afraid not to know what to do.—*a thirty-eight-year-old man*

While the Japanese culture is also an ancient one, the men in that culture express many of the same feelings of discomfort as their American counterparts. The reason, however, is very different. Because arranged marriages remain the norm in Japan, men have not developed expertise in attracting women. A favorite pastime among Japanese men is to go to bars where they pay "hostesses" huge amounts of money to pour their whiskey and listen to them while they get drunk. They will surround themselves with geisha, sometimes four or five at a time, and maybe even have sex with these women when they've become drunk enough, but they seem utterly incapable of courtship or wooing a woman. This comes directly from a culture that teaches them that love is trivial and yet even dangerous (a "temporary disease").

The work I have done in Japan indicates that seduction is a very subtle activity there for both sexes. Women spend a great deal of time making sure their hair is clean. They also pay extraordinary attention to the neck, enhancing its appearance with creams and makeup. Then they will put their immaculate hair up and wear the collar of their kimono to display their neck in the most flattering way. They do this to attract men, and Japan's is the only culture I can think of that does so with a part of the body that has nothing at all to do with the reproductive process.

The discovery sessions on seduction were fascinating all over the world, though they often underscored things I'd already learned. The American sessions were the least predictable, despite what I knew about adolescent cultures. In all, three hundred people from various cities participated in the American sessions, offering me glimpses of not only their first imprint of seduction, but their most powerful memories, and their most recent memories as well. This gave me nine hundred messages to work with—and one very common theme to identify.

The first time my mother told me to keep my skirt down when boys were around. It did not make sense to me at the time. Why not girls, too? Later, I understood.—a forty-five-year-old woman

No idea about seduction. Nothing comes back. Maybe drinking beer with friends, speaking loud, offering a drink to girls, drinking with them. Then going home.—a forty-year-old man

I was going out with an older man. He was nice, but always wanted me to wear a skirt. I thought that was old-fashioned. I like my jeans. Until he told me that I turned him on when I had a skirt. I don't see him anymore.—*a forty-year-old woman*

This kind of angry, confused imagery appeared repeatedly during the sessions—along with stories about "hidden persuaders," subliminal messages, hypnosis, and dishonesty. This was a trait of adolescence I hadn't anticipated: suspicion, fear of being controlled, and rebellion against anyone "telling you what to do."

As I said earlier, emotion is the key to learning. When the emotion that leads to an imprint is a negative one, the imprint is likely to be negative as well. Throughout American society—and the consistency of the responses during the discovery sessions made this abundantly clear—there is a negative association with the concept of seduction. When Americans think of seduction, they think of being forced to do things they don't want to do or that they believe they shouldn't do.

The American Culture Code for seduction is MANIPULATION.

Because we look at seduction in such a negative way, we bring a high level of unconscious suspicion to all relationships between men and women. Even when sexual advances are not confrontational, the unconscious message of "manipulation" is present. Americans invented the concept of the "battle between the sexes." American books and talk shows endlessly exhort their audiences to rail against the way one sex treats the other. Tremendously successful movies illustrate the way men and women manipulate each other during the act of seduction. While these books, talk shows, and movies might use humor to make their points, the underlying message is decidedly unfunny: seduction makes us very, very uncomfortable.

After this discovery, L'Oréal made the decision to work away from the Code in its marketing. While their ads in France were very sensuous and oozed seduction, the last thing they wanted was for American consumers to feel uncomfortable or manipulated when presented with their products. They decided that their advertising would have a distinctly nonsexual spin, focusing on feeling good about oneself. The purpose of using L'Oréal products was not to seduce a man, but rather to feel confident—"Because you're worth it." Their campaigns spoke of feeding and nurturing your skin and hair, evoking unconscious images of motherhood rather than of manipulation.

By avoiding the Code for seduction in their advertising, L'Oréal created a winning strategy. They went "productively off Code." When an advertiser knows that associating a product with a certain Code will trigger negative feelings, it can choose to sidestep that Code completely. Another approach, particularly useful when a negative association is unavoidable (as we will see later with the Code for alcohol), is to subtly acknowledge the Code in such a way as to lessen its impact.

This latter strategy is useful to any individual attempting to be seductive. After all, there is no way to avoid engaging in seduction unless one is resigned to celibacy. A useful tool here is disarming honesty—letting the object of one's affection know of one's interest directly to avoid any sense of trickery or manipulation. The negative Code is still there, but the honesty—the unstated acknowledgment of the Code—will blunt its force.

"AMERICANS DON'T HAVE SEX, THEY HAVE SEX PROBLEMS."
—MARLENE DIETRICH

The adolescent view of the world includes few gray areas. Adolescents tend to see only the extremes: things are good or bad, interesting or boring, meaningful or worthless. This kind of thinking is pervasive in our adolescent culture, and you will see examples of it throughout this book. One such example is the Code for sex.

Knowing the Codes for love and seduction, I approached the Code for sex with every expectation that it would reflect a certain level of discomfort. It was already obvious to me that Americans felt a significant degree of stress when it came to intimate relationships. Still, I did not expect the responses in my discovery sessions to be so extreme.

All boys are dogs. We know what they want. We give it to them . . . sometimes. But we know why they are telling you they love you.—*a fourteen-year-old woman*

When I was eleven years old, I was with my sister, who was twelve, and her friends. We were sitting on the top stairs of an elementary school in our area. My sister's friend told my sister and me about it [sex] because she had just found out about it. It really scared me. I really did not understand the reasoning behind it.—*a forty-two-year-old woman*

I remember I wanted it so badly . . . it was all I thought about for years. But when I finally had sex for the first time, it was over quickly and I felt like someone was scamming me about how great it was. I expected to feel fantastic, but I felt beaten up instead. It was kind of scary how much of a letdown it was. —*a thirty-six-year-old man*

In fifth grade, my friends and I read the book *Are You There God? It's Me, Margaret* [by Judy Blume]. There was talk about sex and I went home and showed my mother, wondering what was happening in the book. She told me for the first time what was going on. I was scared and anxious.—*a woman in her forties*

I was eleven years old and a tomboy when I began puberty. I did not want to become a woman. I was a very serious child and my parents did not prepare me enough for this change in my life. I wondered how I would make it through my teens.—*a fifty-year-old woman*

When I was a teenager, I found out my older sister's best friend was a stripper. After that, every time I saw her, I just wanted to tear her clothes off and have sex with her instantly. My hormones were raging.—*a thirty-four-year-old man*

Repeatedly, the respondents spoke of winning and losing, of taking things and of having things taken from them, even of dominance and being dominated. Even when they wrote about sex as a pleasurable experience, the story often ended darkly.

When I read what people write during discovery sessions, I look not at what they say (remember, you can't believe what people say), but at the common messages. I don't look at the context, but at the grammar. Not the content, but the structure. In doing this with the pieces people wrote about sex, I noticed something in the cadence of the writing; in the regular appearance of words like "scared," "scary," and "anxious" and of phrases like "I felt beaten up" or "I wondered how I would make it"; in the use of clipped sentences and a certain breathlessness in the tone. It brought to mind confrontation, but not the kind of confrontation that is resolved peacefully, with both sides coming away winners. Rather, it brought to mind the kind of confrontation that always has at least one loser and often two. A violent confrontation.

In fact, the American Culture Code for sex is VIOLENCE.

This illustrates the extremist thinking of an adolescent culture. Since we are uncomfortable with sex, we equate it with the extreme opposite of pleasure, something that causes pain and death. It is also clear that as a culture we are far more comfortable with violence than with sex. We consider it bad manners to discuss sex at the dinner table, but we permit lengthy conversations about war, crime, or the latest action movie. If a man is planning a hunting trip with the express intention of shooting and killing something, he can tell all his friends and coworkers and maybe display pictures of himself next to his "prize." If, however, two unmarried colleagues plan a sexual encounter at a nearby hotel, they are likely to tell no one other than their closest confidants. The FCC fines television stations for showing women breast-feeding (as though that were in any way sexual), but on any given night, those same stations can broadcast simulations of murder and mutilation without penalty.

You might recall the 1989 movie *The War of the Roses*. The film chronicles an extremely acrimonious divorce between a character played by Michael Douglas and one played by Kathleen Turner. By the end, their battle turns into all-out physical conflict and the combatants topple off their foyer balcony and crash to the floor below. As the two lie dying, Michael Douglas turns to Kathleen Turner and asks, "Was it as good for you as it was for me?" This sexual question at the end of a fatal confrontation is decidedly on Code. What the director, Danny DeVito, and the screenwriter, Michael Leeson, understood was that Americans have unconsciously "replaced" sex with violence. Our popular culture is filled with the sex/violence connection. Hip-hop lyrics regularly extol the virtues of rough sex. There's an entire subgenre of romance novels called romantic thrillers, in which lovers connect in the midst of stories about serial killers, mass murderers, and terrorists. And how many times have we seen that film cliché where couples slap each other's faces before falling into each other's arms?

It isn't difficult to find places in our culture where the lines between sex and violence blur. Men talk about "nailing" or "banging" a woman when they bed her. Women joke about castrating a man if he cheats on them. Date rape drugs proliferate on high school and college campuses. We commonly refer to singles bars as "meat markets." All this is very familiar.

Earlier, we saw how L'Oréal chose to avoid the negative messages associated with seduction in their marketing. The Code for sex is another negative one, yet American marketers use sex to sell products— very successfully—all the time. When advertisers sell with sex, they tap into the Code. While most of them don't realize, and would be stunned to learn, that they are associating their products with violence, this works for one simple reason: Americans are fascinated with violence. Consider this snapshot: for the week ending October 9, 2005, the number 1 television show in the country was *CSI,* a drama filled with grisly crime images. Number 2 was *Desperate Housewives,* a show about sexy suburban women with several subplots that involve murder. In fact, each of the top five shows that week had strong violent themes. The same week, the number 1 movie in the country was *The Fog,* a horror film; number 4 was *Flightplan,* a violent thriller; number 6 was *Domino,* an action movie about a female bounty hunter; and number 8 was *A History of Violence.* The number 1 DVD rental was *The Amityville Horror,* and the number 2 and number 4 CDs were gangsta rap albums. Americans may abhor real violence, but we find simulated violence enthralling. This is another offshoot of our cultural adolescence: as adolescents, we feel immortal, indestructible, and we are drawn to violence to test our invincibility. When marketers use sex in advertising, they connect with this fascination.

STUCK ON THE ROLLER COASTER

Cultures change at a glacial pace. We will not see the end of our cultural adolescence in our lifetimes. Nor will our children or their children. That means the Codes for love, seduction, and sex will be the same generations from now—not the best legacy. Adolescence is a roller-coaster ride, though, and you will see in subsequent pages how our cultural adolescence, which takes us to uncomfortable lows, leads us to some extraordinary highs as well.

Chapter 3

LIVING ON THE AXIS
The Codes for Beauty and Fat

L ife is tension. Everything we experience in life lies somewhere on an axis between two extremes. One cannot truly know pleasure without knowing pain. One cannot legitimately feel joy without having felt sorrow. The degree to which we feel an experience depends on where that experience lies on the axis (a little painful, overwhelmingly joyful, and so on). The same system that communicates pain to your brain also communicates pleasure, as every sadomasochist already knows.

Similar tensions define cultures. Every culture is composed of an endless number of archetypes and of the tensions between each archetype and an opposing one. For example, one of the primary tensions in the American culture is the one between freedom and prohibition. We consider freedom an inalienable right. We have fought numerous wars to protect it, and our citizens are willing to die to maintain it. At the same time, however, our culture is very strongly inclined toward prohibition. We believe we shouldn't drink too much, play too much, or exhibit too much wealth. While the axis itself never changes, where a culture stands on a particular axis varies from era to era. At various times in our history, for example, our culture has found itself in different places on the freedom–prohibition axis (leaning heavily toward prohibition in the 1920s and far in the opposite direction during the late 1960s and early 1970s), but the opposing force was always evident (bootleggers in the 1920s, the Silent Majority in the latter period). This tension is a constant in our culture and it helps make our culture what it is.

The same archetype in a different culture can have a different opposing force. In France, for example, the archetype on the other side of the axis from freedom is not prohibition; it is privilege. Throughout their history, the French have vacillated between periods when a privileged class ruled the day and periods when this class is overthrown and the nation abolishes privileges and titles. The most famous example occurred, of course, in 1789, though it is interesting to note that Napoleon began a new era of titles and privilege not long thereafter. Today, France has again shifted on this axis toward freedom, but there is still a very real tension, as a result of the Communist Party's espousal of many of the tenets of privilege (minimal or no work, government responsibility for financial welfare, and so on). The French strictly enforce a thirty-five-hour workweek and have six weeks of paid vacation a year, free medical care, and free education. It might be a shock to the French themselves to hear me describe this way of life as aristocratic, but while the *content* of the behavior has changed, the *structure* is very consistent with aristocracy: the notion that working is bad and beneath any person of worth. Though there are few actual aristocrats in France any longer, the undercurrent of privilege still exists, as exemplified by a system where you receive more money in unemployment benefits than you can in many jobs.

When Disney launched Euro Disney in Paris, they learned how much privilege means to the French culture. Originally, the theme park had the same rules as all other Disney parks, barring pets, smoking, and the consumption of alcohol. The French stayed away in droves because they didn't like such restrictions. Disney broke through to the French market only when they began to offer special "privilege passes" that allowed access (for a premium price) to certain parts of the park where visitors could take their pets, smoke, and drink wine. The idea of islands of privilege in a sea of equality was right on Code for the French.

BEAUTY AS A BALANCING ACT AND A NOBLE PURSUIT

When Cover Girl (a division of Procter & Gamble) hired me to find the Culture Code for beauty in America, the tension related to this archetype emerged in my very first discovery sessions.

Female participants, raised in a culture where the unconscious Code for sex is VIOLENCE, consistently told stories whose unspoken message was that one needed to strike a balance between being attractive and being provocative. They gave the clear impression that a line divided being beautiful and being *too sexy*, and that if they crossed it, they put themselves in danger.

Certainly, there are messages supporting this notion throughout the American culture: a judge deciding a rape victim provoked her attacker with her appearance or her actions, for example, or the slashing of a model's face because her assailant thought she was too perfect. American women therefore navigate an axis between beauty and provocativeness, coming as close to crossing over as they are comfortable without actually doing so. Unconsciously, they compile a list of rules to follow: high heels are fine at a social function, but too sexy for the workplace; a tight-fitting, low-cut dress might be acceptable at a private cocktail party with your husband, but if you're single and you wear it to a bar, you're on the prowl; bold makeup can work for a night on the town, but if you wear it to the supermarket, expect some sidelong glances. One of the reasons Victoria's Secret is such a successful company is that it offers women an easy way to navigate this axis: they can be as feminine and sexy as they want *underneath* their clothes, the secret side. Lingerie is the safe way to be beautiful and provocative at the same time. In fact, the name of the company itself suggests the axis, the tension. On one side, we have "Victoria," suggesting Victorian rigidity and repression; on the other side, the "Secret," the hidden closet, the forbidden expression of sexual attraction and beauty.

Uncovering this tension told me a great deal about the perception of beauty in this culture. Being a woman in America is difficult. I often joke (though I am only half joking) that if I am ever reincarnated, I hope I don't come back as an American woman. While I admire American women greatly, I wouldn't want to have to go through what they go through. So many rules; so many tensions.

Understanding the tension was only part of my task for Cover Girl, however. In order to discover the Code, I needed to dig deeper into the stories, to ignore what the participants said in search of what they really meant.

I was about fourteen and I was invited to this big party. I knew that I needed a new outfit. I really wanted to look good. There was a guy that I kind of liked. So I asked my mom for some money for my outfit. I went to the store and found just what I was looking for. I tried this outfit on and I looked hot. I danced all night with this guy and we started to date. I felt that this new outfit did the trick for me.—*a woman in her fifties*

Last summer. On vacation with my family. Ten pounds thinner than usual. Great haircut and color, good skin, manicure, pedicure, summer tan. At a deck party, I danced with my husband on the deck. I felt young and in love. My husband couldn't keep his eyes off me. He said he was proud to be with me.—*a forty-two-year-old woman*

The only time I can remember looking good is when I remarried eighteen years ago to a wonderful man after being alone for seventeen years due to an unhappy marriage. Unfortunately, he died three months after that wonderful experience. I have not felt that I look that good at all since.—*a sixty-five-year-old woman*

My most powerful experience of looking good was when I was fourteen—got breasts, my period, the whole thing. I fell in love with a very nice guy that was five years older than me. My whole world changed.—*a woman in her thirties*

I was three or four years old and my mother's cousin came to visit us. He made a great fuss over my smile and how happy I always was.—*a fifty-three-year-old woman*

In 1970, I met a man named Charles and we started dating. On one date, we went into the city for dinner. It was July and I had been going to the beach so I had the greatest tan. I had gone to a new beauty parlor that day and my hair was perfect. I wore a hot-pants outfit. I walked next to Charles with my shoulders back, my hair flowing, and I felt like a movie star.—*a fifty-six-year-old woman*

My lover made me a thirtieth-birthday party. I wore a lacy black dress. Before the party, there was excitement and anticipation. I looked good and I was loved. I felt cherished. I was the most special person to one other person.—*a thirty-six-year-old woman*

The responses from the hundreds of participants in this discovery revealed something very poignant about the way American women regard beauty. When asked to go back to their first and most powerful memories of their own beauty, they recalled moments of romance, of attraction, of getting a man's attention. Feeling beautiful was associated with dancing all night with a special man, with a brief, wonderful marriage, with falling in love, with feeling like a movie star, and with feeling cherished by a lover. Many of the stories revealed something even deeper. Statements such as "He was proud to be with me," "He made a fuss," and "I was the most special person to one other person" suggested that beauty not only attracted a man, but also changed him in a substantial way at the same time. A large majority of the stories women told about feeling beautiful related to finding a man—and a large majority of those talked about finding men who were life partners, not quick flings. The men who noticed these women weren't slavering slobs, but people with strong, substantial feelings. There was something very powerful here.

Men are programmed for sex and, as much as he might protest this, the average man is willing to have sex with just about any woman willing to have sex with him. If a man notices a woman's beauty, though, if he stops to admire her physical magnificence rather than simply throwing her over his shoulder, his soul is elevated to another level. If a woman can impress her beauty upon a man permanently, if she can stay beautiful in his eyes, she can make him a better human being. She is doing more than keeping herself visually appealing to him: she is elevating him from a rutting animal to something more exalted.

The Code for beauty in America is MAN'S SALVATION.

Think of the hugely popular and enduring film *Pretty Woman*. In that movie, Julia Roberts played a prostitute hired by a hardhearted tycoon played by Richard Gere. While she looks like a hooker, she's nothing more than a plaything to Gere. However, when he needs her to accompany him to a formal function and when she dresses elegantly and makes herself as beautiful (rather than provocative) as possible, she wins Gere's heart. She saves him from a life of emotional emptiness.

Another even more blatant sign of the Code at work in popular culture is with the TV show *Baywatch*. In this series, gorgeous women (most famously Pamela Anderson) perform the function of lifeguards, literally saving men (and women, too, of course) from drowning and other dangers of the water. These women perform heroic acts while appearing as though they have run into the bay straight out of the *Sports Illustrated* swimsuit issue.

Other cultures have different standards for beauty that relate to their own cultural Codes. Among the Arab nations, there are many different cultures, but they share many similar traits because of their common origin as desert nomads. One of these similar traits is the way they regard beauty. They see a woman's appearance as a reflection of her man's success. If a woman is skinny, this suggests that her husband doesn't have the means to feed her properly. Therefore, Arab men want their women to be obese, the better to serve as walking billboards for the men's wealth.

In Norway, beauty is a reflection of one's connection with the natural world. Norwegian men consider slim women with athletic builds the most beautiful, because they see them as active and capable of running and skiing long distances. Norwegian women wear very little makeup and do very little with their hair because naturalness is the most beautiful thing in this culture.

THE BEAUTIFUL LIFE

The combination of the American Code and the tension in this culture between beauty and provocativeness can be a little overwhelming for women. They need to be beautiful to save the men in their lives and thereby to elevate and perpetuate the species; at the

same time, though, they can't be *too* beautiful, because that is dangerous. If they have a bad hair day, are they letting down their entire
species? If their dress is too short, will this lead to man's perdition
rather than his salvation?

The American tension behind beauty is an adolescent one. Adolescents live extreme lives; they are either up or down, invincible or easily defeated. The Code for beauty is man's salvation, but the other
side is perdition. The thing that can save you can also damn you. This
is a very powerful tension.

Fortunately, looking at beauty through the new set of glasses provided by the Culture Code actually makes the axis a little easier to
navigate. Supermodels, for instance, are very much on Code because
they uphold an unattainable standard for beauty. Women can aspire
to that level of perfection without feeling any pressure to achieve it.
Why? Because men—the very men they are trying to save with their
beauty—look at supermodels and say, "I'll never be with a woman
like that." Supermodels are almost like benevolent members of an
alien race. They are fascinating to watch and we can sometimes glean
useful tips from them, but they are not *among us.* On the other hand,
prostitutes and women who dress in outrageously provocative ways
are completely off Code because they suggest to men an easy way to
fulfill their baser desires.

Recently, Dove launched a series of ads for its firming lotion
showing larger and averagely proportioned women in their under-
wear. The message behind the campaign is that this is a "real" product for "real" women. While the media has lauded the campaign for
relating to women in a genuine way and showing them that they don't
need to be supermodels, it is off Code. When beauty is normalized,
when it's suggested that every woman looks beautiful just the way she
is, the elevated nature of beauty is lost. If every woman can be an advertising model, then can anyone save your husband? It's one thing
for models to look like "the girl next door" when a girl that beautiful

actually exists in very few neighborhoods in America. It's another thing entirely when the model can literally be your neighbor. The Code tells us there is considerable mystique surrounding beauty. If that mystique becomes average, something is lost.

FAT IS A SPECTATOR SPORT

Years ago, Tufts University invited me to lecture during a symposium on obesity. My spot in the program came relatively late and I listened to the other lecturers while I waited my turn. It was a distinguished group of speakers speaking to a distinguished and brilliant group of attendees—a room full of M.D.s, Ph.D.s, and a wide variety of other accomplished professionals. The crowd was also substantial in other ways. At least a third of the people in the audience were obese and easily two thirds were overweight.

Lecturer after lecturer offered solutions for America's obesity problem, all of which revolved around education. Americans would be thinner if only they knew more about good nutrition and the benefits of exercise, they told us. Slimming down the entire country was possible through an aggressive public awareness campaign.

I found the juxtaposition of these prescriptions and the round bodies filling the room humorous. When it was my turn to speak, I couldn't help beginning with an observation. "I think it is fascinating that the other speakers today have suggested that education is the answer to our country's obesity problem," I said. I slowly gestured around the room. "If education is the answer, then why hasn't it helped more of you?" There were audible gasps in the auditorium when I said this, quite a few snickers, and five times as many sneers. Unsurprisingly, Tufts never invited me to lecture again.

When I was a young psychotherapist, a woman came to see me with her overweight teenage daughter. The woman wanted me to find out what was "wrong" with the girl and to get to the psychological root of her eating problems. I spoke with the mother and daughter together and then had several sessions with the girl alone. In these private sessions, the girl told me she had no problems with her weight until she reached puberty and began to develop breasts. It was at that point that her mother's boyfriend began making unseemly advances to her. The boyfriend stopped hitting on her only when she got fat. As far as the girl was concerned, everything was now fine.

I met with the mother privately and told her what her daughter said about her weight gain and its relationship to the boyfriend. The woman was aghast, called me a dirty old man (even though I wasn't old at the time), and canceled our future sessions. She took her daughter to a doctor, who put the girl on a strict diet. The daughter's weight dropped dramatically. Unfortunately, the mother didn't get rid of the boyfriend.

About a year later, I was surprised to see an appointment with the girl and her mother on my calendar. They came to see me again because, even though the girl's weight was no longer an issue, the mother had new concerns and she grudgingly acknowledged that I might be able to help. Her daughter now had eczema all over her body. It turned out that after she lost weight, her mother's boyfriend resumed his lecherous ways—until the skin disease turned him off again. My advice to the mother was the same: dump the guy. Sadly, her response to my advice was also the same. I never saw the mother or daughter again.

Fat is a significant issue in this country. More than 125 million Americans are overweight. More than 60 million Americans are obese. Nearly 10 million Americans have been clinically diagnosed as *morbidly* obese. This is excellent news for the diet industry, but alarming news for the rest of us. Regardless of how one feels about body image or definitions of beauty, there are significant health risks associated with being overweight. Contrary to the opinions of those esteemed panelists at Tufts University, most of us know this. The issue, however, persists.

Why are so many of us fat when we know fat is bad for us? Because fat is not a problem. Fat is a solution.

Psychologists have been aware for a long time that fat is an answer to a problem rather than a problem itself. Overeating is a common coping mechanism for the sexually abused. My adolescent patient became fat because her unconscious understood that doing so made her less attractive to her mother's disgusting boyfriend. When her mother essentially forced her to lose weight, her unconscious came up with another answer.

If nearly 50 percent of this country is overweight, there must be a cultural reason for it. What are we coping with? After all, the percentage of overweight Italians is half the percentage of overweight Americans, and a recent *New York Times* best-seller proclaims that *French Women Don't Get Fat* (not true: actually; nearly a third of French women are overweight, though that is still dramatically less than the 62 percent rate of overweight among adult women in America).

As always, the stories participants told during the third hour of our discovery sessions were revealing. Some spoke of triumph:

> After battling with an extra twenty pounds or so for my height, I became very depressed, especially while shopping. It was a nightmare because the clothes never fit right and I wouldn't even dare to check out myself from behind. I made a pact with myself to finally lose the weight before it "got too late." I took off thirty or so pounds and felt very proud and successful.—*a twenty-two-year-old woman*

> When I was twelve, I decided that I must go on a diet because I was starting to be interested in boys and they weren't interested in me. I went on a diet of cottage cheese and fruit and lost twenty

pounds! I was so happy, and my cousin Nancy, who was quite slim and older than me, gave me some of the shorts she had out-grown and they fit me perfectly. I remember our next-door neighbor telling my mother I was too skinny. That was great!
—*a woman in her late fifties*

Some spoke of tragedy:

When I was about a second-grader, my paternal grandmother was diagnosed with adult-onset diabetes. She was born and raised on a farm and lived her adult life as a farmer's wife. She cooked with lard, butter, and real cream. At the noon meal, she typically put three meats, four or five starches, four to five vegeta-bles, and three desserts on the table . . . and she ate like a farmer. She was five feet tall and weighed over two hundred pounds. She died of complications associated with her diabetes, in a way eat-ing herself into the grave.—*a thirty-five-year-old woman*

I was young; first grade, I think. I was shopping with my mom for my school uniform and the top was too tight around my arms. I remember feeling bad and "less than" in some re-gard. I felt like a bad person because I was bigger than my friends. Right around this time, my dad died and that just con-firmed my bad feelings. I was fat. I was bad. My dad died. There-fore, I was not good enough and I was being punished in some respect by having my father taken away.—*a thirty-eight-year-old woman*

Some spoke with sadness:

My cousin was a beautiful young girl. Slim, porcelain skin, blue eyes, and white-blond hair. She was very rebellious, though, and made some bad choices that messed up her life. I had not seen her for some time until this past spring. She is now extremely obese with barely distinguishable facial features. I was saddened to see this change and more distressed when I saw that her three children were obese as well.—*a forty-five-year-old woman*

I remember a family bike ride when I was about four or five. My dad, brother, sister, and I were active. My mom rarely did things with us actively because of her size and discomfort. I recall that she looked silly upon the small seat of the bike. She seemed uncomfortable with the whole experience. I would have liked to have made her thinner and therefore more comfortable in clothes, going out, being more active.—*a woman in her fifties*

When I was young, I moved to a new house. Before I moved, I was not overweight. When we moved, I kept myself inside away from the other children because I was upset that I had moved away from my friends. I stayed in the house that whole summer and because I stayed in, I gained weight. I wish I could change that summer because I might have changed the way I am today.—*a man in his late thirties*

Others spoke with anger:

Recently I went dancing and there was a man I met who was fairly interesting to me. I looked at his stomach and he was fat, which is a real turn-off to me. I was not interested in him. I feel repulsed by a man that is fat. I could never be attracted to him. It's one of the first things I notice about a prospective suitor. —*a sixty-one-year-old woman*

I remember walking home from school with my little sister when I was in sixth grade. Some kids called her "fatty," and the tears in her eyes made me mad enough to chase one of the boys and give him a bloody nose. She has had weight problems ever since.
—*a forty-nine-year-old woman*

Something connected all of these stories and the hundreds of others like them. It didn't matter whether the participants told of clothes or farms, bicycles or bloody noses. What did matter was the way they spoke about these things. Losing weight and being thin made people "feel proud and successful" at how their clothes "fit perfectly." Being overweight, on the other hand, related to "being punished," "keeping inside," and being "a real turn-off."

The axis of tension emerged via these stories. Just as the other side of the axis from beauty for Americans is provocativeness, the opposite position on the axis from fat is connection. As a culture, we believe that thin people are active and involved. They are "proud and successful" and their clothes "fit great." On the other hand, fat people, according to the stories, are disconnected from society. They turn people off, they stay inside, and they fail to interact with their families.

This axis is visible everywhere in this culture. A woman might stay thin through the early years of her marriage, but after her second or third pregnancy does not lose the weight. Why? Because she is unconsciously disconnecting from her husband in order to concentrate on being a mother. A man struggles uncomfortably with a life in middle management and, when he puts on an extra thirty or forty pounds, complains that he has been passed over for a promotion because of his weight. People balloon multiple sizes after a bad breakup, the loss of a job, their kids' departure for college, or the death of a parent.

The tension is always there. We might use alibis, like "big bones" or a slow metabolism. We might talk about "love handles" or how true beauty resides "on the inside." Quite often, though, those of us who struggle with our weight are also struggling with one of our connections—to loved ones, to the roles we play, to the "rat race."

The Code for fat in America is CHECKING OUT.

Al Gore never served as president of the United States, but he serves as a visual representation of the Code. When Gore lost the 2000 presidential election, he was understandably distraught and he dropped out of sight for a few months. When he finally agreed to give an interview, we saw him sporting a beard and a considerable amount of extra weight. The loss was so devastating to him that he checked out. Interestingly, when he recently held a press conference to announce the launch of his new cable television network, he looked trim and fit. Al Gore had a new purpose; he'd checked back in.

Given such a Code, is there any question why there are so many overweight people in this culture? As Americans, we are masters at putting undue pressure upon ourselves. We must be supermoms. We must climb the corporate ladder. We must have a relationship worthy of a Harlequin romance. That's an awful lot to handle. In fact, for many of us, it's much too much. Therefore, we unconsciously check out. Better to blame the fat than to acknowledge our desire to eschew expectations.

Getting fat is the most common available unconscious way to check out of the rat race, to adopt a strong identity (as an overweight person) without having to fight for it, to move from active to passive. Being fat allows us to know who we are (fat), why this has happened (the overabundance of food "forced" on us), who is responsible (McDonald's or some other fast food restaurant that "makes us" eat their food), and what our identity is (a victim). Fat also allows us to use commonly accepted alibis to regress to childhood. Another tension we experience is that as babies and young children, we are fed with the intention of making us fat—no one wants a skinny baby—but as we get older, society pressures us to be thin. If we get fat enough, we unconsciously think, perhaps others will take care of us again, as they did when we were babies.

In other cultures, fat sends a very different message. In the Eskimo culture, fat is a sign of hardiness. If one is fat, one can make it through the terrible winters when food is scarce. In the English culture, fat is a sign of vulgarity. The English cultural trait of detachment extends to overeating. If you watch English men and women at a buffet table, you'll see them approach the table with indifference and choose very little to put on their plates. From their perspective, to do anything else is vulgar, and anyone who overeats so often as to become fat is a vulgar person.

CHECKING OUT OF CHECKING OUT

Understanding the Code allows us to address our weight issues in much more profound ways than eating bacon cheeseburgers without bread, purchasing exercise equipment that rusts in our basements, or consuming huge quantities of "negative-calorie" foods before bedtime. Nor is the answer simply good nutrition and an active lifestyle, although both are vital to maintaining health. Before we can conquer the *solution* of fat, we need to answer one fundamental question: from what am I checking out?

Acknowledging that one eats when one is stressed, depressed, or otherwise overwhelmed by the world is definitely on Code. If one understands that stress leads to "checking out," one can pay more attention to the underlying problem. Does eating make the problem go away? Does excess weight remove you from the circumstances that cause the problem (by, for example, making you unappealing to the opposite sex, or turning you into the wrong "type" for that big promotion)? Do you really want this solution?

While one might argue their nutritional wisdom, fad diets are on Code because they offer consumers something to check in to. Embarking on a diet like Atkins or South Beach is a bit like joining a club with a huge number of members. When these diets are at the apex of their popularity, they are the topic of conversation in kitchens, supermarket lines, coffee shops, and cocktail parties all over the country. Participants in these diets can "check in" to a large subculture of other people losing weight this way, giving them a sense of connection. Of course, these diets have little long-term value for most people because they don't address the reasons people checked out in the first place. As the Code has shown us, loading up on carbs is a solution; too much pasta is rarely the real problem.

One company that does an especially good job of dealing with fat is Weight Watchers. Like the fad diets, they offer a sense of membership to their customers, including regular meetings. Like diet books, they also offer eating plans and nutritional advice. In addition, though, they offer counseling sessions to help members deal with their weight issues and (though Weight Watchers doesn't put it this way) the reasons they are checking out.

This approach is totally on Code.

THE PURSUIT OF SALVATION

Side by side, the Codes for beauty and fat give us a glimpse into something deeper than how we regard physical appearance in America. If you're beautiful, we've seen, you're performing a noble mission; if you're fat, you're checking out of your role. We celebrate beauty, are awestruck by it, aspire to it. On the other hand, we discriminate against fat people and marginalize the morbidly obese, even though overweight women make up the majority of the female population in this country and the number of people who are overweight in America is higher than the number who voted for both candidates in the

2004 presidential election. Our new glasses let us see something that most of us have observed but few truly understand: how central to our culture is the pursuit of salvation. We will explore this further when we discover the Codes for work and money in America and when we reveal the Code for America itself.

Chapter 4

FIRST COMES SURVIVAL
The Codes for Health and Youth

All human beings are born with brains divided into three parts. One part, the cortex (the cerebral hemispheres), handles learning, abstract thought, and imagination. The cortex comes into practical use in most children after they are seven years old. Before that age, children do not have the mental tools to make intellectual assessments. If you take two identical balls of clay and ask a child, "Are they the same?" the child will say, "Yes." If you roll one of the balls into the shape of a snake and ask the child which piece of clay is larger, however, the child is likely to pick one or the other. Ask the same question of a child older than seven, though, and he or she is likely to say, "Do you think I'm dumb or something?" The cortex is where logic resides and where we do the higher-level reasoning that separates us from all other animals.

Another part, the limbic system (the hippocampus, the amygdala, and the hypothalamus), deals with emotions. Emotions are never simple; they are often rife with contradiction. In a business context, for instance, when customers tell you they love you, this is good, right? What if they love your products and never buy them? Would you rather have them hate your products and buy them all the time? The limbic brain is structured between birth and age five, largely through a child's relationship with his mother. From her, we receive warmth, love, and a strong sense of connection. It's very rare to experience that with a father. Because of this relationship with the mother, the limbic has a strong feminine side—when we say a man is "getting in touch with his feminine side," what we're really saying is that he is not afraid to access his limbic brain. Most humans find that in the struggle between intelligence and emotion, the limbic often comes out on top, as we are much more likely to allow our heart to guide us than reason.

The undisputed champion of the three "brains," however, is the reptilian brain (the brain stem and the cerebellum). The name comes from this region's similarity to the brains of reptiles, which are believed to be relatively unchanged from the brains their predecessors had 200 million years ago. Our reptilian brains program us for two major things: survival and reproduction. These are, of course, our most fundamental instincts: if we could not survive and reproduce, our species would end. The reptilian brain is therefore more influential than our other two brains. Physical attraction, for instance, has a strong reptilian dimension. At the reptilian level, one is physically attracted to someone whose genes provide the best chance of survival for one's progeny in one's circumstances. This is why, as previously discussed, an Eskimo man is more likely to find a round, overweight, tough woman attractive. At the reptilian level, he believes she has a better chance of surviving the harsh winters and brutal living conditions of the Arctic. If the Eskimo man in question combines his genes with hers, his children will have a better chance at survival.

Because survival is more fundamental to our existence than "feeling good" or "making sense," the reptilian brain always rules the day. In a battle between logic, emotion, and instinct, the reptilian brain always wins. This is true when one is dealing with personal welfare, human relationships, purchasing decisions, and even (as we will see later in this book) the choice of leaders.

Like individuals, cultures have a very strong reptilian dimension.

One can look at a culture as a survival kit passed down from one generation to the next. The American culture evolved as it did because the pioneers, and later the waves of immigrants who came to our shores, needed it to evolve that way if they were to survive the conditions of this vast country. Traits such as Puritanism, a strong work ethic, the belief that people deserve a second chance, and putting a premium on success all helped us to survive in this new world. Eskimo culture is decidedly different from American culture because the survival conditions are decidedly different. Swiss culture evolved the way it did, forging multiple cultures into one very strong one, in response to regular threats to Switzerland's survival as a sovereign state. One can trace the distinctive evolution of each culture on the planet to the survival needs of that culture.

Thus, we find the Codes for the elements of a culture when we understand how our reptilian brains address that element. This process is especially clear when we look at the Code most closely related to survival—health—and the Code for youth.

WHAT I LEARNED FROM THE WITCH DOCTORS

Maintaining health and helping the sick has always been a passion of mine. This is the "healer" side of me, my feminine anima. Because I wanted to understand healing from as many perspectives as possible, I spent two years in the late 1960s studying witch doctors in Nicaragua. Afterward, I went to Bolivia and explored the difference between white magic and black magic. Finally, I spent several months in the Mato Grosso, an affluent area of the Amazon, to study with a *curandero,* a witch doctor–healer.

Before this sojourn, I was already aware that science had limits, that things happened in our brains and our bodies that we hadn't been able to explain via the scientific method. These years in South America brought me to a new level of understanding. Some of these witch doctors were great psychologists. For example, they would not start healing a patient unless the patient proved he really wanted to be cured. One witch doctor I studied sent his patients on initiation journeys deep into the forest to find special plants and fight imaginary demons and monsters—all to prove his dedication to overcoming his disease. This same witch doctor refused to treat a patient unless his entire family was committed to the cure and played a part in the initiation journey. There is powerful logic behind the witch doctor's actions. He wanted to make sure that the patient was in the best frame of mind to get better, that he felt he could conquer the disease, and that his family was strongly behind him. This might seem like medical common sense, but how many "traditional" doctors prepare their patients so completely before attempting a cure?

This witch doctor found a way to "detach" his patients from their cortexes. He didn't bring out medical texts or send his patients to WebMD to read up on their diseases. Instead, he appealed to their reptilian brains. The witch doctor convinced his patients that he could help them survive—as long as the patients wanted it enough.

I'LL TAKE THAT LIFE TO GO

When Procter & Gamble hired me to discover the Code for health and wellness in America, I saw this as a very exciting opportunity because health is, of course, one of the primary archetypes of life. I therefore expected to uncover a Code that spoke to the essence of what it meant to be alive in this culture.

Americans are doers. In the words of that great American philosopher Nike, one can boil the American agenda down to three simple words: "Just do it." Our champions are athletes, entrepreneurs, police officers, firefighters, and soldiers—all people who take action. We may respect thinkers, but we don't celebrate them nearly as much as we do our action figures. It isn't accidental that, for years, at the top of the stairs of the Philadelphia Museum of Art—a repository of great works of intellect and imagination—there resided a bronze statue of a famous cinematic boxer. Can one imagine a monument to Jackson Pollock standing outside Yankee Stadium?

This culture-wide call to action informs the way we look at our health. Few of us find it important to maintain the conditioning of a Navy SEAL or a marathoner (in fact, given the obesity figures in the previous chapter, many of us seem to find little need to maintain any conditioning at all), but we strongly believe that we need our health in order to *do things*.

During the ten discovery sessions I held over the course of this study, I received different kinds of stories. There were those that told of illness:

When I was eighteen, I learned that my grandmother, who had raised me and always taken care of everyone, was dying of lung cancer. This just didn't seem possible. She was eighty years old, walked several blocks every day—to the doctor, to the grocery, anywhere she wanted to go. She was the strongest woman I've ever known. She lived almost eighty-one years and for all but the last two weeks, she wasn't dependent on anyone.—*a forty-six-year-old woman*

When I was eight, the doctor told me I had a lack of calcium in my left leg and couldn't put any weight on it. My mom and dad had to carry me everywhere. Every month, the doctor looked at my leg through a fluoroscope and my mother looked over his shoulder to see how my leg was coming. I hated that my mother had to carry me everywhere.—*a sixty-five-year-old man*

I remember being ill when I was five. I had to stay in bed in a darkened room. The curtains and venetian blinds were closed to keep out the light. I had to rest my eyes, which meant not reading books or watching TV. I was so very bored. Being declared well at last was like getting out of jail! I couldn't wait to go outside.—*a woman in her forties*

A few years ago, I contracted a case of gout—imagine that; a person supposedly in the prime of his life who stayed in good shape and was careful about what he ate suddenly getting gout. My right big toe swelled enormously and every step was painful. I hobbled around like Walter Brennan and I felt like I was a hundred years old.—*a forty-seven-year-old man*

There were those that told of recovery:

When I was a child, an accident left my mother paralyzed from the waist down. The doctors told her she would never walk again. She spent sixty-one days in the hospital trying to deal with her paralysis and how to care for four children all under the age of six. After she got home, she was depressed all the time, but one night my grandmother took her to church and a preacher told her God was going to heal her. She didn't believe it, but that night, she walked up the driveway without any help. The doctors couldn't believe it, but she is still walking today, twenty-four years later.—*a thirty-year-old woman*

My mom is doing better in her battle with breast cancer. It was hard seeing her down and she looked older. Now she is always on a cruise or a vacation. It's great seeing her alive again.—*a twenty-nine-year-old woman*

There were those that offered the participant's personal definition of wellness:

> My most powerful experience of wellness came a few weeks after college graduation. I had a job lined up and a few weeks before I had to begin work. I went on a road trip with close girlfriends from college in an old orange VW Bug. One day, I was behind the wheel and my other friends were asleep. I was lost in my thoughts, driving in the country. Suddenly, I was filled with a wonderful feeling as I turned a corner on the road—I realized my whole life was ahead of me and it was going to be fantastic.—*a forty-five-year-old woman*

> My most recent experience of wellness came when I was hired for my new job. I feel a sense of satisfaction being in a job where I feel appreciated after being unappreciated at other companies. I feel like I have an impact on others.—*a forty-five-year-old man*

> I was about eleven or twelve years old when I started to have a feeling of wellness. My parents' divorce was in the past. It was hard, but my mother found her sense of independence and maybe it rubbed off on me or something. It was a springlike day and I was roller skating by myself. The air was soft and fragrant. At this moment, I felt the power of the universe and my own power.—*a forty-six-year-old woman*

> A glorious week at Rancho La Puerta in Mexico. The first time in my life I have taken time for myself. No job. No kids. No husband. Just meditation, yoga, African dance, morning walks, a step class, and a massage every day.—*a forty-two-year-old woman*

Regardless of the kind of story a participant chose to tell me, a powerful theme emerged. There was clearly more to health and wellness than not being sick. Health wasn't about being hale enough to enjoy a sunny day or spend quiet time with your spouse. Being sick wasn't about a cough or a cold, or about aches and pains. What these participants told me was that being sick meant that someone needed to carry you, that you were not allowed to play outside, that you hobbled around, and that you couldn't walk to the grocery. Recovery meant walking up the driveway or taking a series of trips. Wellness was associated with long drives, roller skating, doing a job that had an impact on others, or African dance.

For Americans, health and wellness means being able to complete your mission. The mission might be running a multinational corporation, getting the kids off to school, participating in local politics, scaling a mountain, or cooking a great meal for your family, but it involves *action*. As the message within these stories indicates, Americans believe that if they are strong enough to act, then they are healthy. Their greatest fear about being sick is the inability to do things.

The Code for health and wellness in America is MOVEMENT.

If we put on the new glasses provided by this Code, certain behaviors in our culture stand out. Why do we fill up our free time? Why do retirees begin second careers? Why are we so devastated when, as we become elderly, we lose our driver's licenses or find ourselves relegated to wheelchairs?

The answer is in the Code. Though we might have a stressful job, a demanding family life, and a bevy of obligations, we still take up golf, learn to knit, join a gym, or even start a book group. These acts involve various forms of movement, and movement makes us feel healthy, confirms that we are alive.

This is why retirees, after long, intensely active careers, feel lost when they give up their jobs. It is a very reptilian response. They can *intellectually accept* the notion that they've worked long enough and saved a sufficient amount to remain comfortable. They can *feel* a sense of relief when they realize they no longer need an early alarm clock. Their reptilian brains tell them something else, though: things have slowed down—maybe too much. Many of them suddenly find themselves with much less to do—with much less movement in their lives—and the prospect is frightening. Some seek comfort and health-affirming movement in hobbies or organizations. Some plunge into hypochondria and depression, feeling that the lack of movement in their lives suggests that their health is failing. Others take the most active path to solving this problem: they unretire. A second career restores a sense of movement and therefore returns their sense of good health.

The Code also explains why the loss of movement is so devastating to us. Seniors will battle mightily to avoid life in a wheelchair, often struggling for years with a walker before acceding. Similarly, they will make every effort to retain their driver's licenses, giving them up only when they prove to be a danger to themselves or others. Why? Because this loss of movement makes a very dramatic statement about one's health, and this permanent change toward a less mobile state suggests that health will never return.

In other cultures, the concept of health takes on a different dimension. For the Chinese, health means being in harmony with nature. Chinese medicine has been around for five thousand years and has always taken into consideration the human being's place in the natural world—curing illness using plants and herbs, astrology, and even the phases of the moon. The Chinese believe that they live in permanent connection with the natural elements and that good health is related to being at peace with nature.

The Japanese, on the other hand, see good health as an obligation. If you are healthy, you are committed to contributing to your culture, your community, and your family. The Japanese are obsessive about remaining healthy, and they feel a powerful sense of guilt if they fall ill. Unlike our culture, in which children will fake fevers (via the old thermometer-to-the-lamp trick) or stomachaches to get out of school, Japanese children will apologize to their parents for getting sick, for they know illness may cause them to fall behind. In this culture, you don't just wash your hands to stay clean, but also out of a sense of duty to yourself as a servant of the culture and to prevent someone else from getting sick because of you.

DOCTORS, NURSES, AND THE MEAT GRINDER

The Code for health sheds interesting light on some related Codes. Doctors and nurses are charged with keeping us healthy. Given the strength of our reptilian instincts, it is unsurprising that we have very positive Codes for both.

The stories told during discovery sessions for the American Code for doctors projected images of rescue, of being saved from danger, of being spared a horrible fate. Most Americans were imprinted with the notion that doctors save lives and can recall a time when a doctor saved a family member, or maybe even a time when a doctor saved them personally. The Code for doctors in America is HERO.

Our feelings about nurses are even more positive. A recent Gallup poll identified nursing as the most ethical and honest profession in America for the fifth time in six years (it ranked second to firefighting in 2001, in the aftermath of 9/11). We perceive nurses as caretakers, as the professionals who spend more time with us when we are sick than our doctors do, and who *always* have our best interests at heart. Discovery stories included phrases such as "made me feel better," "came in and sat with me," and "I wanted to believe her." Americans feel safe and loved with nurses at such a high level that there is really only one comparable relationship. The Code for nurse in America is MOTHER.

We think of doctors as heroes and nurses as mothers. Therefore, we must have a positive impression of every component of the medical field, right? Actually, no. The Code for hospitals is starkly (and darkly) different. Few places in the world evoke more reptilian feelings than hospitals. We are born there, we die there, and our futures often depend on the tests and procedures that take place there. Hospitals inspire a sense of foreboding by filling their halls and rooms with scary-looking equipment, a sterile, impersonal environment, and air that smells antiseptic and artificial. Discovery participants told stories worthy of Poe in our sessions. Words like "probe" and "impersonal" came up regularly, and we read phrases like "being rushed to the operating room to die" and "some carcass they were experimenting on." The unconscious connection we make with hospitals is that when we are there, we are not people, but rather products. The Code for hospital in America is PROCESSING PLANT.

The hospital Code seems shocking in light of the Codes for doctors and nurses—but not when we remember that the Code for health is movement. Hospitals inhibit movement. We need to stay in bed. We have tubes and machines connected to us that keep us from getting around. When we're allowed to walk at all, we have to do so slowly, attached to an IV pole. And if we're lucky enough to get out of there, they don't even let us leave under our own power, instead insisting that we be wheeled to the curb.

Movement is the key to our attitudes about all of these. Doctors and nurses get us moving again and we love them for it. Hospitals keep us pinned down and we think terrible, terrible things about them.

KEEP ON MOVING

From a business standpoint, the new glasses provided by the Code offer essential insight to any company seeking to market health or a healthy lifestyle. Positioning a product in this arena as something that

promotes movement, mobility, or action is right on Code. A good example is GMAC auto insurance. When one calls GMAC after an accident, the representative's first question is "Can you move?" This
acknowledges the unconscious connection between movement and
health and, if the caller *can* move, it reassures him that he's probably not too badly injured. Interestingly, the next two questions
from GMAC address the other parts of the brain. The first is "How
do you feel?" The next is "Can you give me the details of the accident?" The questions follow the hierarchy from reptilian to limbic to
cortex.

Any product that suggests constraints on movement is off Code. A
national retail chain recently launched an ad campaign using the
tagline "Contain yourself." I cringed. While the store sold products
that every American home could use, their message was completely
wrong for the American unconscious. We *never* want to be contained.
We might want to contain our clutter, our old "stuff," or our off-
season clothing, but containing *ourselves* has no appeal at all.

THE YOUTH OF AMERICA IS THEIR OLDEST TRADITION. IT
HAS BEEN GOING ON NOW FOR THREE HUNDRED YEARS.
—OSCAR WILDE

The Code for health in America sends a very optimistic message
about the way we perceive our personal futures. We believe that if we
live active, engaged lives, we will stay healthy. As long as we have
something to do, we will remain strong. Interestingly, though, the discovery sessions for youth in America revealed a darker message, one
created by the collision between our reptilian instincts and our cultural adolescence, that leads adults to play a sometimes unhealthy
game of dress-up.

Our reptilian brains program us for survival. People in every culture want to survive. In the American culture, however, we not only

want to survive, we want to remain at the peak of our powers. It is not nearly enough to be an active old person in America. We want to retain the illusion of invincibility that every teenager has. Americans are fascinated with youth and the fanciful notion of staying young forever. *Time* magazine dedicated the cover and a significant portion of its October 17, 2005, issue to the topic of aging well and remaining young. Bob Dylan offers us his wish that we stay "Forever Young," while Frank Sinatra tells us "fairy tales can come true, it can happen to you, if you're young at heart." A hugely popular film like *Cocoon* fantasizes an alien force that can turn the elderly young again, while *Logan's Run* imagines a "utopian" world where one is not allowed to live past the age of thirty.

As we saw in chapter 2, Americans are eternal adolescents. We look at Europe as the old world and America as the new. Yet in many ways, America is one of the oldest of the world's nations. The French Revolution began in 1789, more than a decade after our own revolution. Modern Italy became a nation-state in 1861. The German empire was founded in 1871. Our *culture* isn't nearly as old as the French, Italian, and German cultures (all of which existed long before the current nations of France, Italy, and Germany), but we have existed in our present form longer. We have the oldest written constitution in effect on the entire planet.

So why are we so fascinated with youth? One reason is certainly that we are a culture filled with immigrants. Immigrants come here and leave the past behind. They start over in America. They are reborn here, often with new careers and new (American) dreams. Since we continue to receive immigrants in large numbers, this sense of renewal and reinvention is a living thing in our culture. In itself, this keeps us young.

In addition, because we are an adolescent culture, we tend to think like adolescents, even when we are in our sixties. We don't want to have to grow up. We don't want to settle into adulthood. We regard electronics equipment and automobiles as "toys," and we have coffee dates with our "girlfriends" even when those "girls" are grand-mothers.

Since youth in America is as much a state of mind as it is an age, the sessions to discover the Code for youth in this culture included people of all ages. Despite the varied nature of the groups, however, the third-hour stories had very similar structures:

> Staying young is critical in my office. My boss is only twenty-nine and he's always talking in sports metaphors and referring to our competition as "graybeards." A few months ago, I joined a gym for the first time in ten years so I could drop some pounds and chisel a few muscles. I put in an hour and a half four times a week. I feel like I'm training for a marathon, but if I want to stay in the game, I have to have the look.—*a forty-four-year-old man*

> My husband and I came home from my birthday dinner and I discovered my first gray hair. Within a week, I found dozens more. Then some wrinkles that I know weren't there before. I al-ways told myself that I would keep a "natural look"—as little makeup as possible and no hair dye. I couldn't keep that prom-ise, though. The thought of watching myself get old in the mir-ror scared the heck out of me. I bought some Clairol and got a makeover at Macy's. It might be fake, but it makes me feel bet-ter.—*a thirty-two-year-old woman*

> My teenaged grandson loves the fact that I played drums in rock bands in the late fifties and early sixties. My son never thought this was a very big deal, but his son wants to be a drummer too and he asks me all kinds of questions. I started listening to some of Greg's music and I found I really liked it. I even listen to it in the car and I find myself pounding away on the steering wheel.

Rock and roll always made me feel young and this new music gives me that feeling all over again.—*a sixty-year-old man*

I had my first child when I was in my early twenties. When my daughter was a teenager, it tickled me when people would refer to us as sisters. I was a very cool mom and I went out of my way to keep up with what my daughter was interested in and the hottest trends. Last year, my daughter had a baby and people started calling me grandma. I am *so* not a grandma! I love that little boy and would do anything for him, but grandmas are gray and puffy and overweight. I told my husband recently that I was thinking of having my grandson call me Joan rather than grandma. He laughed at me. I still might do it, though.—*a forty-nine-year-old woman*

For years, people greatly underestimated my age. People in management referred to me as "kid" when I was nearly forty. A couple of years ago, I had some medical problems and I wound up in the hospital for a month. When I came out, I couldn't get around as fast as I once did, and the weight I lost made me look gaunt and older. I don't know if it's just my imagination, but all of a sudden, people around the office started calling me sir. As soon as my doctor cleared me to do so, I went on an all-out program to get myself back into shape. People still don't call me "kid," but they will again someday.—*a forty-seven-year-old man*

I've always had a vision of myself as the way I looked the day I got married. I had porcelain skin and huge eyes and shimmering blond hair. People actually gasped when I walked down the aisle. I was the epitome of the young bride. I always thought I looked that way, even as the decades passed. A couple of years ago, my husband died. When I got home from the funeral, I looked at myself in the mirror and saw a gray lady dressed in black. I couldn't figure out where the old woman in the mirror came from. I try to avoid looking in mirrors now.—*a sixty-three-year-old woman*

I love being young. How can you not love it? You can do anything you want, your entire future is in front of you, guys look at you and like what they see. I plan to stay young for a very long time, and I'll do whatever it takes to do it. I read some article that said that some day soon scientists will have a vaccine to stop aging. I'll be the first person in line to get that shot.—*a twenty-year-old woman*

In these stories and the hundreds of others like them, people spoke of youth as something tangible, something that could be kept or recaptured: "I have to have the look." "It might be fake, but it makes me feel better." "People still don't call me 'kid,' but they will again some day." "I'll be the first person in line to get that shot." They felt they could create the illusion of youth if they listened to youthful music, wore makeup and dyed their hair, or imagined themselves at a certain age rather than looking in the mirror. For Americans, youth isn't a stage of life, but something you can hide behind, something you can wear instead of your actual age.

The American Culture Code for youth is MASK.

There is evidence of the youth-mask connection everywhere in our culture. Plastic surgery literally pulls our faces tight around our skulls, as though we were putting on rubber masks. Botox freezes our facial muscles into a masklike countenance. You can even buy "anti-aging masks" to remove wrinkles and beautify the skin. In fact, since our impression of physical youth is so often related to the face and head (the skin and the hair), one could say that any attempt to look younger is a version of wearing a mask.

Just as a costume mask creates an illusion, so does the mask of youth in our culture. As Barbara Walters homes in on her eightieth birthday, she maintains the appearance of someone decades younger. Is Joan Rivers seventy? Fifty? One hundred? It's hard to tell through her mask. When we say that Paul Newman looks great at eighty, we're really saying that he's done an excellent job of masking his age. We don't think he looks great because he looks eighty; we think he looks great because he looks considerably younger.

Many other cultures are not nearly as fascinated with youth as we are. Hindu Indians believe there are four distinct stages to one's life. Youth is the first and least interesting, something to pass through quickly as you gain the tools necessary to live in the world. The next stage, maturity, is when you have children, make money, and achieve success. The third stage is detachment. Here you step back from the world and the "rat race," choosing instead to read and explore philosophy. In the fourth stage, you become the equivalent of a hermit. One will often find elderly Indians roaming the streets covered in ashes, looking as if they've passed on to the afterlife already. In the Hindu Indian culture, a person graduates from one stage to the next, with death being the ultimate graduation. Hindu Indians don't fear death, and the notion of fighting off aging is ludicrous to them.

The English find youth boring. Young people are inexperienced and prone to mistakes. The English regard young people as children who must be tolerated. Where Americans glorify the vitality and verve of youth, the English glorify the same qualities in their eccentrics. A key tension in England is the one between detachment and eccentricity. While the culture practices detachment, it revels in the other side of the axis. How else to explain the knighting of a man who famously wore a duck suit to work (Sir Elton John), or of another who launched a new product line by shaving his beard and dressing in drag (Sir Richard Branson)?

DRAPING US IN YOUTH

Marketers operate on Code when they present a product as something that can give consumers a "mask" of youthfulness. Just for Men positions its hair-coloring product as something that "targets" gray hair and masks it with tones approximating one's natural hair color. The company's on-Code ads show a man masking his gray in just five minutes and then enjoying a full, youthful life.

With men, hair is the key to youthful appearance. Sometimes this means removing the gray. At other times it means regrowing hair that was once lost. Though bald men from Yul Brynner to Michael Jordan have stood as sex symbols in this culture, *balding* men rarely share that spotlight. Rogaine has done an excellent job of on-Code marketing by selling its product as something that can mask male-pattern baldness by enabling you to grow new hair and therefore appear more youthful.

Hair is part of the mask of youth for women as well, of course, and Pantene markets its shampoo and hair products in an on-Code way. Pantene ads concentrate not on cleanliness, body, or luster, but instead on health—essentially telling consumers that Pantene products keep hair young. The ads speak about strengthening and feeding your hair, treating it like a young child that needs nurturance to grow. Recent ones even tap into the Code for health as movement by saying that Pantene products give hair "swing." For a middle-aged woman seeking youthful hair, this is a powerful message.

Another effective way to market a youth "mask" is to sell a product as youthful even while your core market is something else. Mazda introduced the Miata as an entry-level sports car for young people. The company continues to position the car that way more than a decade later (its website includes a Miata video game), even though the largest group of owners is over fifty-five years old. Sticking to this strategy is very much on Code and has proven very successful for

Mazda. The company appeals to its most active buyers by suggesting that the Miata offers the mask of youth.

The French mime Marcel Marceau does a very funny routine in which he pantomimes putting on a mask of a smiling face. A minute or so into the routine, he attempts to take off the mask and finds that it is stuck. As he struggles and writhes to free himself of the mask, the smile remains plastered to his face. At the end, he slumps, defeated, but his synthetic smile is still there. In many ways, our obsession with youth is like that mask. Artificial treatments such as plastic surgery, Botox, and hair replacement give us the luster of youth, but they come at a high price and are often accompanied by pain and discomfort. Peppy cars and youthful clothing are exciting and wonderful if we really connect with them, but can make us feel like frauds if we employ them only to create the illusion of youth. Understanding the Code allows us to step back to answer some important questions. Do I really want to go through life wearing a mask? What would happen if I took it off? Am I missing something by hanging on to youth rather than embracing and exploring maturity? Since America is a youth culture, the answers to these questions are predictable. The new glasses of the Code allow us to see a different reflection in the mirror, but only for a moment.

AFTER 200 MILLION YEARS, IT KNOWS A THING OR TWO

The Codes for health and youth are powerful examples of our reptilian brains at work. These Codes express themselves this way in our culture because we see them through the prism of our particular survival kits (we will address this further when we talk about biological schemes and cultural schemes in the next chapter). Given the need for our ancestors to build an entire country, we don't think of health as merely freedom from disease but rather as the ability to accomplish things—to keep moving—and to continue to contribute late in our lives. Since our adolescent culture has no reverence for the elderly, we feel the need to mask our aging and create the illusion of being forever young.

Our cortexes might tell us that aging brings us wisdom. Our limbic systems might suggest that health is a matter of taking a positive outlook and feeling good.

When our reptilian brains speak, however, we have no choice but to listen.

Chapter 5

MOVING BEYOND THE
BIOLOGICAL SCHEME
The Codes for Home and Dinner

As mentioned earlier in this book, every species is distinguished by the structure of its DNA. I call this the biological scheme. In addition, every culture has a cultural scheme
that is an extension of the biological scheme. The biological scheme
identifies a need, and the cultural scheme interprets it within the parameters of a particular culture. "Isomorphism," a term borrowed
from biology, chemistry, and mathematics, is commonly applied to the
continuum between the biological scheme and the cultural scheme.

For example, our human biological scheme dictates that our physical comfort peaks within a certain air temperature range. If the air is
too hot, we become lethargic. If it is too cold, we run the risk of illness and, in the extreme, death. To address the heat issue, we developed air conditioning. Each culture, however, regards the use of air
conditioning differently, depending on its cultural scheme. Americans
consider air conditioning a necessity (virtually every car in America
comes equipped with an air-conditioning system), while Europeans
consider it a luxury (in the UK, air conditioning is not standard
equipment even on a Rolls-Royce). I recall visiting a four-star hotel in
Germany a few summers ago. My room was very hot; when I asked
the concierge to address the problem, he told me that the hotel didn't

have air conditioning because the weather only got this hot one month a year. This might have been sensible from their perspective, but as an American, I found it uncomfortable. It had an unpleasant impact on my stay and I kept thinking that even a room in an inexpensive motel in the United States would have had a temperature more to my liking. The German hotel's policy was appropriate for the human biological scheme, but not for my American cultural scheme.

On the other hand, I regularly hear Europeans complain that American stores are too cold in the summer. Again, the conflict lies in the cultural schemes. Americans like to be cool, even extremely cool. Research has shown that the coldest stores in America tend to be the most expensive. Since air conditioning is a necessity, we need *extreme* air conditioning to convey a sense of luxury.

Biological schemes are specific to each species, and are not negotiable. We breathe with our mouths, noses, and lungs rather than with gills. These biological schemes pre-organize the way a Culture Code is created and evolves. They establish the parameters within which a particular culture can survive. A culture that spends some of its time underwater can work. One that spends *all* of its time underwater cannot. As long as a culture acknowledges the limits of biology, however, it is free to roam within the parameters. We all need to eat, but the American culture created fast food while the French created slow food. Every species needs to reproduce itself, but some cultures employ polygamy (one man with several women) while others prefer polyandry (one woman with several men). These are cultural answers to the same biological scheme.

One biological scheme is the need for shelter to protect us from the elements. Our first home is the womb. After that, each culture takes over, adapting to its natural environment (igloos for Eskimos, tents for nomadic Arab tribes, and so on). Once this biological need is met, the cultural scheme may evolve within a particular culture. By looking at the American Culture Codes for home and dinner, we can see where our culture has taken this evolution—how *house* became *home*.

NO PLACE LIKE HOME

Americans address the biological scheme when they build their houses: roofs and insulated walls protect us from weather and extremes in temperature, HVAC systems keep us cool and warm, kitchens allow us to feed ourselves, and bathrooms provide a place to relieve ourselves. We go far beyond the biological scheme, however, when our houses become our homes.

Home is a tremendously powerful archetype in the American culture. One of our most sacred, most distinctively American rituals—Thanksgiving dinner—is all about coming home. The dinner most often takes place at the residence of the family matriarch; even if she has moved over the years, and even if you yourself never lived in that house, it represents home. When we gather for Thanksgiving dinner, we reconnect with our homes and affirm the importance that home has in our lives.

When our troops go off to war, we offer them support and encouragement, but from the very beginning of the engagement, our goal is to "bring our boys home." Some of our most enduring and powerful images are of soldiers returning to our shores and into the arms of their loved ones. In fact (as has been reinforced by the recent war in Iraq), our sense is that, regardless of what is accomplished along the way, a war is not truly won until our soldiers come home.

This notion shows up even in our national pastime of baseball. It isn't coincidental that this American sport includes three bases and a *home* plate. Home is a potent and pervasive image for us, and baseball illustrates that eloquently: the only way to score is to make it home.

The powerful icon of home is pervasive in American pop culture, from commercials for Folger's coffee to Hallmark greeting cards to songs that promise our return to our lovers. Perhaps no piece of contemporary entertainment better captured the resonance of this icon, however, than the Ron Howard movie *Apollo 13*. If this was a movie about any other space mission (let alone a space mission that failed in all of its initial objectives), the moviegoing public would have shrugged. After all, we'd long since expressed our boredom with the space program and initiatives to return to the moon, live in orbit, or send shuttles to and from a space station. *Apollo 13* was a huge blockbuster, however, because it was about something else entirely, something much closer to our hearts: bringing people home.

There are obvious reasons why home means so much to Americans. This country was founded by a group of people who came here to create a new home. When they arrived, there were no houses, no roads, none of the trappings of home. For most of them, there was also no turning back. For political, financial, or logistical reasons, they could not return to the place they left behind. This was even truer for the waves of immigrants who followed them, people who gave up everything they owned for a chance to start a new life in the New World. These people turned their backs on everything they knew and came to America in search of home. In doing so, they defined home not only for themselves but for the entire culture they created.

Americans may have a stronger sense of home than any other culture on the planet. We see home not only as the house we grew up in or the one where we live with our families, but as our entire country. No invading force has ever occupied our country. Never in our history have we lost our home (as opposed to most other countries around the world that have been occupied or annexed at some point). The French do not share this sense of home. After multiple invasions, the French sense of "homeland" is considerably less intense than the American sense. (This, by the way, is one of the reasons people from other countries are simultaneously fascinated and repelled by Americans' strong sense of nationalism.) Many other countries were stitched together from various cultures after a war (Iraq after World War I, for instance) or, like India, gained independence after long years of colonial rule. These countries do not have the same sense of the country as their home that we have.

What mental highway do we traverse when we think about home? What unconscious signal do we receive? I explored the Code for home for Homeowner Insurance Company, but I also received many insights from studying other subjects, such as corrugated boxes (for Inland Container) and coffee (for Folger's).

My first memory of home was my mother's picking me up from the bus stop after my first day at school. I was very nervous about going to kindergarten and even though that first day turned out better than I expected, I was still so glad to see her waiting for me when I got back. We went home, had a snack together, and talked about the day. From then on, we did that every day until I went to high school.—*a twenty-four-year-old woman*

When I came back from my first semester at college for Christmas break, I had a big party at my house for all of my friends. I don't think I realized how much I missed these people until I saw them all again. Some of us stayed together until four in the morning just getting back in touch.—*a thirty-six-year-old man*

We had this thing in our home every Sunday dinner. Before we ate, we told each other our highs and lows for the week. Sometimes the things we talked about were really silly, but a lot of times we talked about things that really meant something. I tried to be home for dinner every Sunday night because I really loved having the chance to bounce things off the other members of my family.—*a thirty-two-year-old woman*

It's funny, but when you asked me to think about home, I think about seeing my parents and grandparents in the stands watching my Little League baseball games. For some reason, knowing they were there to root for me made me feel at home even when I wasn't home.—*a twenty-six-year-old man*

Things were always a little disjointed when I was growing up. My father lived in Cleveland and we only saw him during the summer. My mother worked late and really couldn't spend a lot of time with us. Now that I'm happily married and have my own family, though, I find that home has a completely different meaning to me. We have all of these little rituals associated with holidays and birthdays and even the start of baseball season. It seems that we find lots of different reasons to celebrate being together.—*a forty-year-old woman*

My father died five years ago. Family was so important to him and he gave me a very strong sense of home. He was my rock and I miss him like crazy. Even today, whenever something is bothering me or even when I have great news, I talk to this picture I have of him on my kitchen counter (yes, I know that's a little weird) and it makes me feel like he's still with me.—*a woman in her sixties*

The language in these stories reveals strong emotion, exactly what one would have expected given the subject. The emotion had a definite sense of motion, though, a surprising emphasis on repetition. Coming back from school and sharing a snack every day. Coming back from college and finding the old friends with whom you once spent so much time. Sitting down over dinner to share stories every week. Seeing your family at every game. Sharing rituals. Seeking advice and comfort from a family member who had died. There were many words that could describe the message triggered by the sense of home—but only one prefix.

The Code for home in America is the prefix "RE-."

When we think of home, we think of words that begin with the prefix "re-." Words like return (as the girl did when she came home from school), reunite (as the boy did when he got back from college), reconnect (as the family did when they told each other their highs and lows for the week, and as the woman did when she spoke to the picture of her father), reconfirm (as the boy did when he saw his family in the stands at his baseball games), and renew (as the woman did during her family's various rituals). This sends a very powerful message to us about what it means to be home. Home is a place where you can do things repeatedly and have a good sense of the outcome—unlike the outside world, where everything can be so unpredictable. Home is a place where doing things *again* gives them added meaning. This is why coming home has such a powerful dimension in this culture and why we have such a strong emotional reaction when we think about bringing home our troops or our endangered astronauts. We want them to experience their lives again, surrounded by the people who mean the most to them.

Home has different meanings in other cultures. Because space is at a premium, the Japanese consider every inch of the home precious. The Japanese remove their shoes before entering their homes to avoid sullying their treasured space with dirt from the outside. Each room has multiple functions (the living room becomes the bedroom as futons [invented by the Japanese] are converted from seating space to sleeping space) and few people in Japan have a room of their own. Interestingly, there is no word for intimacy in Japanese. When one lives in such close quarters, the concept goes without saying.

Nomadic Arab tribes are always moving. Still, they have a very strong sense of home, even though it is not related to a specific place. They have tents made of camel hair that are incredibly gorgeous and intricately designed. When they make camp, they appoint their tents luxuriously with items that have strong personal meaning—beautiful furniture and carpets—which they take with them from place to place. The first time I entered one of these tents, I was amazed. The family I visited had its entire culture under one roof.

In the American house, the kitchen is the central room where the family gathers. Contemporary kitchens include televisions, desks, islands with stools for seating, and other amenities that promote congregating. The kitchen is the heart of the American home because an essential ritual takes place there: the preparation of the evening meal. This is a ritual filled with repetition and reconnection that leads to replenishment. Making dinner is on Code for home in America.

Having grown up in France, I found my first visits to American homes a little surprising. I would often enter the house through a side door or even the garage and walk directly into the kitchen. There I would be told to "help myself" while the meal was prepared in front of me. This was very alien. In France, houses are designed differently and visitors are entertained in another way entirely. The biggest rooms in a French house are the "stage" areas: the foyer, the living room or salon, and the dining room. Guests will have drinks and coffee in the salon and dinner in the dining room and they will never see the kitchen. This is true even among close friends.

Knowledge of the Code explains a great deal about why "going home" means so much to us, even after our families have moved to a house where we never lived. If home is about return, reconnection, renewal, reunion, and other words with the prefix "re-," then the physical location means nothing. What is important is that the feelings and family exist wherever you define "home." Keeping our mementoes, photo albums, and symbols of home life is on Code because these things allow us to return to a sense of home whenever we need it. Throwing out memories to remove clutter is off Code. Having Thanksgiving dinner in your grandmother's crowded dining room is decidedly on Code, while going to a roomy but unfamiliar restaurant for the holiday is not.

For businesses, awareness of the Code offers clear-cut ways to market household products. The Betty Crocker people came to me years ago to discover the Code for the icon of Betty Crocker herself. They believed that the icon had outlived its time and that if they understood the unconscious messages Americans received from the icon, they could reinvigorate their brand with new symbols. Instead, they learned that the image of Betty Crocker has a very strong positive imprint on the American unconscious. The American Code for Betty Crocker is THE SOUL OF THE KITCHEN. She represents tasty aromas and hot food. She has a very strong place in the American perception of home.

The Betty Crocker brand managers changed their plans completely. Instead of jettisoning the icon of Betty Crocker, they relaunched it. They gave the "new" Betty Crocker a face that appealed to all races. They gave her a distinctive handwriting and a voice to speak on radio (where she offers homemaking advice).

Selling any household item with the notion that it can become part of a family ritual (anything from popcorn to coffee to laundry detergent) is a valuable way to ignite our affection for home. Cell phone companies offering free calls to family members are on Code because they promote reconnection. An airline or travel agency that offered special packages for family reunions would be right on the mark.

When I worked with GMAC Home Insurance, we learned that at the unconscious level Americans believe that home is where their "stuff" is. We discovered, for instance, that people will pack a box of personal goods during a move, put it in the basement, and then move that same box—never opened—from new home to new home. The content of the box is unimportant (and often unknown). What *is* important is that the box contains "stuff," and "stuff" has great value in making Americans feel at home. Because of this work, GMAC home insurance is exploring a program of preserving family photos—very important "stuff"—for policyholders. They would keep digital files of these valuable photos and replace them if they are destroyed in a fire. This resonates in a very on-Code way.

WHAT'S COOKING? ANYTHING?

Like the need for shelter, the biological scheme for dinner is fundamental: all human beings need nourishment. But what is the continuum between the biological requirement to eat and the particular cultural scheme in America? Like the notion of home, the concept of dinner is very powerful in our culture.

Dinners have a strong ceremonial place in America. That biggest dinner of the year—Thanksgiving dinner—even commemorates the launch of our culture. We commemorate holidays and birthdays with large family dinners; the celebration dinner is one of the most common ways to mark an accomplishment, such as a promotion or a good report card.

Each of these dinners is a major event that can produce lasting memories. What imprint comes from the everyday dinner, though—the weeknight meal one shares with family (at least occasionally) after a long day of work or school? Kraft, wanting to learn how to make its products synonymous with American meals, was interested in the answer to this question, and commissioned discovery sessions to learn what dinner means in America. Later in this book, we will decode food in general, but here the focus is on the meal that, as we will see, has the most resonance in the American mind.

In the first hour of these sessions, we heard what people think about the average dinner. It was something to prepare quickly. The family rarely sat down to eat together because everyone had such a busy schedule. When they did sit down together, there was often a TV playing. The meal consisted of a takeout pizza or a pre-prepared entrée. Conversation consisted of a fast debriefing on the day and then silence. The meal was over in fifteen minutes or less.

Certainly, none of this was surprising. Americans, who equate health with movement, have very active lives. We work long hours. We have soccer practices and tennis lessons and book clubs and poker nights to attend. We have three hours of homework, or a pile of papers brought home from the office. We have shows to watch and instant messages to write. Where are we supposed to find the time to prepare a nice meal or to linger over it with the clan? I got the sense during these first-hour conversations that Americans thought of the family dinner as a quaint element of our past, like the sewing circle or the ice cream social.

When we got to the third hour of every session, however, and when the harried participants relaxed and thought back to their first, their most powerful, and their most recent memories of dinner, the meaning of this meal bore no resemblance to what they'd said earlier.

Some spoke of regular family gatherings:

I always looked forward to dinner every night. First of all, my mother was a great cook, so we always had something good to eat. Even if she just threw something together quickly, it tasted fantastic. But the other thing was that everyone got to sit around and talk to each other. My parents, my two brothers, and I discussed the day's events and upcoming plans for the following day. It was a warm environment, full of love and nurturing. Everyone was given an opportunity to speak about anything important to them. It was the time that everyone had to check in with each other.—*a twenty-seven-year-old woman*

I used to love coming home from school and watching reruns of old TV shows. Once, when I was ten or eleven, the station playing *The Honeymooners* moved it to 6:30. I was totally hooked on that show and asked my mother if I could eat dinner in the den rather than eating with the rest of the family. I could tell this hurt her feelings, but she told me I could do it, so I did. That night, sitting in the den with my food, I found the show wasn't that funny. I could hear my parents talking in the dining room and I felt like I was missing out on something. The next night, my mother asked me if I was eating dinner in the den and I told her I was going to eat with the family. When we sat down together, my mother patted me on the hand and said, "Welcome back."—*a forty-one-year-old man*

Everyone had a specific place around the table. My little brother sometimes tried to sit in my chair and I would nearly tear his head off. We ate off of plates we made at one of those paint-your-own pottery places and we always ate at 6:45 because my dad came home at 6:30. When my brother and I got older, we didn't eat together as often, but we still did it whenever we could. When I went off to college and I ate at the dorm cafeteria for the first time, I got incredibly homesick.—*a nineteen-year-old woman*

My father was a traveling salesman, so we didn't have family dinners all that often. When Dad was home, though, dinner was a big deal. My first memory of dinner was of being maybe five or six. My dad was in a great mood and everyone was joking around. My older brothers were teasing me, but not in the mean way they sometimes could. I remember that moment like it was yesterday. I felt bigger than life because I was surrounded by people who loved and cared for me.—*a fifty-three-year-old man*

Every few months, my father would drive the whole family from Oakland, California, to State Line, Mississippi, to visit my grandmother. All of my uncles and aunts would be there and about twenty cousins and ten from my family (brothers, sisters, mom, dad). The house would be so noisy and everyone would be talking about the old times and we'd eat until everything was gone.—*a forty-eight-year-old man*

Some spoke about life getting in the way:

It seems that my kids got older and my husband started spending time on the road at just about the same time. For a while, I tried to make dinner, but then I realized I was kidding myself. My most powerful memory of dinner is me eating out of a Tupperware bowl at the kitchen table with magazines and mail on it. My dinner companions are mail-order catalogs and bills. —*a forty-five-year-old woman*

My two kids are out of the house now and I don't do much for dinner now that I'm alone. If I could change anything about the past, it would be that I would have provided a more "traditional" meal for my children. I would have insisted they eat with me rather than doing all the stuff they were doing. Time with our children is so short.—*a fifty-year-old woman*

I took a job on the night shift because the money was much better. Unfortunately, that meant I could no longer have dinner with my wife and kids. A sandwich in the cafeteria isn't exactly the same thing as a hot meal at home. One night, my wife surprised me by packing up the kids and dinner and coming to see me at work. The five of us sat around the cafeteria table and it was the best meal I'd had in a long time. I took a little longer than my

usual break and my boss wasn't too happy about that, so we couldn't do it very often, but I loved it when they came.
—*a thirty-nine-year-old man*

Some spoke of the sadness associated with permanent absences from the dinner table:

I'll never forget the first family dinner we had together after my mother died. Dad cooked—it was his job now—and he did the best he could considering how upset he was. Still, when we sat down, it was like someone had cut a huge gaping hole into our kitchen table. The room felt dark and empty. Nobody talked. And the food didn't smell as good, and not because my dad couldn't cook as well as my mom. I remember feeling like the family was going to fall apart.—*a twenty-five-year-old woman*

I truly miss the big gatherings and the love and fun that used to be part of the big family gatherings. Unfortunately, money has broken the family into parts and it doesn't seem that the whole family will ever be together again.—*a thirty-six-year-old woman*

When my mother and father divorced and my father moved to Indianapolis, Mom did everything she could to keep a regular dinner time and to pull us together for dinner. But I could tell that she was really upset that Dad wasn't there anymore. She never really got over it, and dinner was never the same again.—*an eighteen-year-old man*

Sunday dinner was a huge event in my household. It was the one time during the week that my father insisted I be around. My older siblings would come over with their kids and we'd put the extensions on the dining room table, everyone would sit around, and there would be huge plates of food in the middle of the table. My parents spent all day Sundays cooking. Then my brother-in-law got a job in Cleveland and moved my sister and two nieces out there. It was weird, but I knew right away this was the beginning of the end. Six months later, my other sister moved out of town, and a couple of years later I went off to college and then settled in the Bay Area. The only time we get the whole family together now is for Thanksgiving, and it just feels forced.—*a thirty-four-year-old man*

These third-hour stories were filled with deep emotion: the joys of camaraderie, the satisfaction of a warm family environment, the sadness and regret of loss. While Americans might not have family sit-down dinners together very often any longer, these meals have a cherished place in our hearts.

One notion that came up repeatedly was the gathering. "Everyone got to sit around and talk to each other." "Everyone had a specific place around the table." "The five of us sat around the cafeteria table and it was the best meal I'd had in a long time." "When we sat down, it was like someone had cut an enormous gaping hole into our kitchen table." "Everyone would sit around, and there would be big plates of food in the middle of the table." The image that showed up in a huge percentage of the stories was the idea of coming together *around* a table. There is a sense of community generated by this act, the sense that you are surrounded by people who support you and are there for you. You can go out into the world, but when you return for dinner and you sit around the table, you are truly home.

The American Culture Code for dinner is ESSENTIAL CIRCLE.

This notion of a circle expresses itself in multiple ways in the American culture. A common American practice is to serve food "family style," with large plates of food set at the center of the table (creating a circle of sorts, even if the table is rectangular), after which diners pass the plates around the circle so everyone can share. In addition, dinner completes the circle of the day. You wake up in the morning, you leave the house, you go out to do battle in the world, and then, at dinnertime, you return to the family and close the circle with your loved ones.

Dinner has a very different structure in other cultures. A Japanese family rarely eats dinner together. Commonly, the men work all day and then go out to drink with their friends. When they get home, their wives may serve them a little soup before they go to bed, but the children will have been fed long before. The notion of the family meal is relatively foreign in Japan. Even when a married couple goes out to dinner with friends, the men and women eat separately.

In China, dinner is all about the food. Food is cooked in multiple locations (the kitchen, the fireplace, outside, even the bathroom) and it has a hugely prominent place in any Chinese home. Food is hanging, drying, and curing everywhere. While the Chinese are eating dinner, they rarely speak with one another. Instead, they focus entirely on the food. This is true even at business dinners. One may be in the midst of a spirited conversation about an important deal; when the food comes, all conversation ceases and everyone feasts.

Dinner in England is a much more formal experience than it is in America. The English have very clear rules of behavior at the table, including how one sits while eating, how one uses one's cutlery, and even how one chews. One would never see English diners in a restaurant offer a taste of the food on their plate, as Americans commonly do. While Americans see this as convivial, the English see it as vulgar and unsanitary.

IT'S DINNERTIME AND EVERYONE'S INVITED

Gathering together at dinner, completing the essential circle, is absolutely on Code. The desire to do it was stated emphatically in the

discovery sessions. Yet if you ask any head of household about dinnertime in her family, you're likely to hear about one or both parents
grabbing something on the way home from a late night at the office,
one kid pouring a bowl of cereal for herself, and another heating
something in the microwave on his way out the door. This is reality,
right? We're very busy Americans.

Equally interesting is what *is not* implied by the Code. Looking
back at the stories, one notes that participants mentioned food itself
infrequently. In addition, they put no premium on gourmet quality or
on long preparation time (we'll discuss why when we get to the Code
for food). Even the woman who referred to her mother as a "great
cook" said things "tasted fantastic" even if her mother "just threw
something together." The very strong message of the Code is that
the *circle* is the important part of dinner. Food is secondary.
That take-out pizza is perfectly fine as long as everyone is eating it together (interestingly, DiGiorno, a Kraft brand, promotes its pizza as
being as good as takeout, not as good as homemade). Pizza is, in fact,
an ideal, perfect on-Code dinner because it is circular and everyone
shares it.

Once they received the Code, Kraft launched a marketing campaign using the catchphrase "Gather around." They even animated
the Kraft logo to morph into a family sitting around a dinner table.
They positioned themselves as facilitators of the on-Code American
dinner experience.

Another thing not implied by the Code is a sense of duration. Few
participants talked about lingering over dinner with family. Again, the
important thing was the circle. The on-Code dinner is a time when
everyone can gather around the table and reconnect. A fast meal with
the entire family together and the television off is on Code.

A dinner doesn't need to take place around one's own table to be
on Code. Restaurants that promote bringing the family together are
very much on Code. McDonald's did a great job with this when it in-

troduced the Happy Meal. By offering kids something specifically for them, the company made it easy for families to eat together, even if the meal itself was something less than elegant. All "family restaurants" are on Code because they promote gathering the family together for dinner, they offer something for everyone, and they create a casual environment that promotes fun and conversation.

Restaurants that promote community tap into the Code in powerful ways. The Melting Pot, a chain of fondue restaurants with nearly a hundred locations in the United States, does this especially well. Patrons sit in booths that simulate a household dining table, and the food is served in the middle of the table. Fondue is an especially on-Code meal because diners are always reaching into the center of the circle to get food. This produces a sense of sharing even more potently than passing plates around the table does.

Products that promote single servings are off Code for dinner, though they are of course not off Code for our busy lifestyles. Kraft takes a twofold marketing approach with its macaroni and cheese. It sells its Easy Mac brand of single-serving packages as an after-school snack that kids can make for themselves, while it sells its classic Macaroni & Cheese as a dinner that the entire family can enjoy. Stouffer's has an interesting way of keeping the single-serving concept on Code. In its recent advertising for Lean Cuisine, it shows a woman bragging to her female friends about the sumptuous low-calorie meal she had the night before. Essentially, by spreading the word about Lean Cuisine, she's inviting these women into her "circle." Even if these friends don't eat dinner together, they form a community when they eat the same frozen dinners.

HOME IS IN OUR HEARTS

We need shelter and we need to eat. As Americans, we elevate these basic requirements into something involving family and ritual.

When we think about home, one of the first images to come to mind usually involves a big family meal. When we go home to visit our parents, we go home for dinner. Just as the ritual of making dinner is on Code for home, creating a strong home environment is on Code for dinner, even if, in these busy times, dinner itself comes out of a box.

Chapter 6

WORKING FOR A LIVING
The Codes for Work and Money

"What do you do?"

When someone asks you that question, you could offer any number of answers. You might discuss your role as a parent. Or you could talk about the various things you do to maintain your household. You might respond with a list of your hobbies. In America, though, the question really means "What *job* do you do?" and the only expected answer involves your work.

There is something very powerful and revealing about the way we ask "What do you do?" in American culture. It's another way of asking "What is your purpose?" as though one were looking at an unfamiliar machine and asking "What is it for?" We usually ask it almost as soon as we meet someone. "Where do you come from?" is the first question, followed by "What do you do?" The answers enable us to size someone up, as well as providing an evening's worth of small talk.

In several other cultures, one's work is not nearly the passion and preoccupation it is in ours. Stendhal's classic novel *The Red and the Black* defined a French culture in which one's life had value only if one served the country (as part of the military—the red) or God (as one of the clergy—the black). All other occupations were vulgar, best left to peasants. This attitude still pervades French culture and leads to a system in which the unemployed receive more money than many service employees receive. A major best-seller in France is *Bonjour Paresse,* whose title translates as "Hello Laziness."

Most of my European friends are baffled that I continue to work so hard long after I've made enough money to keep me comfortable the rest of my life. To them, the concept of continuing at one's job because one loves one's work is unfathomable. Europeans usually take six weeks of vacation every year. Here, two weeks is the norm, and many people take their work on vacation with them, or even go years without a vacation while they are building their careers.

This has been the American approach to work from the very beginning of our culture. When our forefathers came to America and discovered a huge undeveloped land, their first thought wasn't "Let's have some tea." It was "Let's get to work." There was a New World to create, and it wasn't going to create itself. Towns needed building. The West needed opening. The rudiments of a bold political experiment needed to be put in place. There wasn't time for leisure then, and in a very real way, we still believe there isn't time for it now. Americans work longer hours than the people of any other culture.

Americans celebrate work and turn successful businesspeople into celebrities. Donald Trump and Bill Gates are pop stars. Stephen R. Covey, Jack Welch, and Lee Iacocca are mega-selling authors. Instead of *Bonjour Paresse,* our best-sellers include *The Seven Habits of Highly Effective People* and *Good to Great.* Billionaire owners of sports teams, like George Steinbrenner and Mark Cuban, make the headlines as often as the athletes they employ.

Why does work mean so much to us?

Why do we need to love our jobs?

Why is it so important to us to have a strong work ethic?

When I set out to discover the Code for work in America, I was able to play my role of "visitor from another planet" with unusual credibility. While I myself had an extremely positive attitude toward work and a huge amount of passion for what I did, I grew up surrounded by those who embraced the French attitude. I already knew that Americans took a very different approach to work, but I was curious about how they imprinted this and what it meant to them at an unconscious level.

The "bad focus group" conversations of the first hour of the discovery sessions varied widely. While some participants spoke with excitement and optimism about their jobs, others complained about long hours, low pay, and difficult employers. And while all seemed to agree that work was something you "had to do," their attitudes about this obligation ranged. When we got to the third hour, however, and I asked participants to recall their first imprint of work, a very clear pattern emerged.

I had a paper route when I was a teenager. There were days when I dreaded it—snow was the worst—but for the most part, I had fun with it. I liked collection days, and not only because I got tips. I liked talking to the customers and getting to know them.—*a forty-five-year-old man*

My most powerful memory was just a couple of weeks ago. I'm a camp counselor and I ran into one of my kids at the video store. She saw me and ran into my arms and brought me over to meet her father. When she said, "Dad, this is my counselor," she said it like I was a queen or something.—*an eighteen-year-old woman*

I work three jobs to keep my family going. It seems that the only thing I do is work all the time.—*a forty-seven-year-old man*

I remember my first grown-up job. I worked during the summer in high school and college, but this was totally different. This was a career. I liked having colleagues and taking on assignments and planning out my future. I got a promotion after only six months and I felt like I was on the map.—*a thirty-two-year-old woman*

I worked for the same company for twenty-three years. One day, a bigger company bought them and suddenly I was out on the street. For six months, I kept trying to find a new job and kept getting nowhere. When I wasn't looking for a job, I felt like I had nothing to do. My wife and kids had their lives, but I had nothing. I finally got a new job for much less than I used to make. It doesn't feel the same, and I don't feel the same.—*a forty-seven-year-old man*

My first paying gig changed my life. This was it. I had arrived. I was a professional musician!—*a twenty-nine year old man*

My first memory of work was watching my mother break her back lugging boxes of fruit for her fruit stand. It seemed to me that she was struggling all the time, but she never complained about it. I know she didn't like the long hours and the hard labor, but she liked talking to customers. Everyone knew who she was—she was the fruit stand lady.—*a sixty-nine-year-old woman*

The tone of the stories ran the gamut—people were happy with their work, they hated it, they felt invigorated, disappointed, or overwhelmed—but the energy of the stories moved in a very specific direction. Work put you in a position to get to know people, excite children, keep your family going, or plan your future. Work could make you feel that you were like a queen, that you were on the map, or that you had arrived; work could make you feel that it was all you did; if you lost your work, you could feel that you had nothing.

Though participants might have suggested otherwise in the first hour of our sessions, their third-hour stories gave them away. For Americans, work wasn't simply something you did to make a living or because you had to do it. Even if you didn't like your work, it had a much more powerful dimension, a life-defining dimension.

The American Culture Code for work is WHO YOU ARE.

When we are wearing the new glasses provided by the Culture Code, the question "What do you do?" takes on added meaning. In essence, when we ask someone what she does for a living, we ask her who she is. Americans very strongly believe that they are what they do in their jobs. Why are unemployed people often depressed by the loss of their jobs? Because they are unsure of how they will pay the bills? Certainly. At a deeper level, though, it is because they believe that if they are "doing" nothing, then they are nobodies.

If work means "who we are," then it is perfectly understandable that we seek so much meaning in our jobs. If our jobs feel meaningless, then "who we are" is meaningless as well. If we feel inspired, if we believe that our jobs have genuine value to the company we work for (even if that "company" is ourselves) and that we are doing something worthwhile in our work, that belief bolsters our sense of identity. This is perhaps the most fundamental reason why it is important for employers to keep their employees content and motivated. A company operated by people with a negative sense of identity can't possibly run well.

Ritz-Carlton does an excellent job of giving its staff a positive sense of who they are. The company calls its employees "ladies and gentlemen serving ladies and gentlemen." Their goal is to give their guests the best hotel experience of their lives, and their employees' job is to provide that experience. Ritz-Carlton understands that if they want to create a culture of sophistication for their guests, they need to do the same for those who work there. They treat their staff like adults and give them a strong sense of empowerment. If a cleaning person encounters a guest with a problem and the guest complains to her, that cleaning person has the power to improve his experience by giving him a free meal or even a free night in a room. This gives the cleaning person a strong sense of motivation, the belief that she is part of the corporate mission.

Another component of the Ritz-Carlton management approach is that they refuse to burden their staff with the motto that "The customer is always right." Understanding how humiliating it can be to live by that precept, the president of Ritz-Carlton tells his employees that if someone gets out of hand, to let him or someone else in management know and they will take care of it. Again, this approach fortifies the employees' sense of who they are. It is much easier to treat the guests like "ladies and gentlemen" when you are treated like a lady or a gentleman yourself. Ritz-Carlton employees tend to be very loyal and very proud of what they do.

Effective employee relations in other cultures reflect that culture's attitude about work. In France, work takes a backseat to the pursuit of pleasure. If a job isn't entertaining, most French workers would prefer unemployment. Gerard Blitz adopted this French approach to staff management when he founded Club Med. One of the first things he did was change job titles—for instance, the manager of a Club Med is the *chef du village* (chief of the village). Then he instituted nightly shows at which employees entertained guests. Any member of the staff could go up on stage if he or she had the guts. In addition, when Club Med opened its doors, it positioned itself as a welcome place for willing and adventurous singles. In such a sexually charged environment, the personnel had an excellent chance of sharing in the fun. This camplike atmosphere in a resort setting made work pleasurable for the staff—so much so that Club Med regularly gets away with paying their employees less than the competition.

ALWAYS ON THE JOB

Americans rarely accept a dead end in their jobs without a fight, and they strongly believe that you are only as good as your last deal. A billionaire still works sixty hours a week because he needs constant affirmation of who he is. A recently promoted middle manager ratchets up her work energy because she already has the next promotion in her sights. Our work ethic is so strong because at the unconscious level, we equate work with who we are and we believe that if we work hard and improve our professional standing, we become better people. Remember, the American Code for health is movement; this extends to professional health as well. It is possible to be happy doing the same job for thirty years, but only if that job provides consistent new challenges. Otherwise, we think of ourselves as "stuck in a rut" or "going nowhere." How many people do you know who are thrilled to do the same job on an assembly line or as an office functionary indefinitely?

We're always seeking the next promotion, the next opportunity, the next chance for something big. If you talk to a cabdriver in Manhattan, you're more likely to find that he's going to school to get a better job than that he plans to drive a cab the rest of his life. If you meet a waitress in Southern California, she's likely to tell you that she has an audition for a movie next week. The cabdriver might never get out of his cab and the waitress might be performing a recitation of daily specials for the next twenty years, but the sense that they're moving toward something more glamorous is very much on Code. On the other hand, those who fail to act, who accept the limitations of their work with barely a grumble, are likely to feel miserable about their lives. The hopelessness of their jobs has done critical damage to their identities.

Our new glasses also help explain why we celebrate hugely successful businesspeople. We love the story of Bill Gates laboring away in his garage, coming up with a great idea, and becoming the richest person in the world. Why? Because it reinforces the notion that "who we are" has endless room for growth. The self-made millionaire (or, in Gates's case, "fifty-billionaire") is an inspirational symbol for us because it proves that all of us can work hard, find the thing that we do superbly, and forge an extraordinary identity. Similarly, stories like those of Tom Clancy (a middle-aged insurance salesman who became an enormously popular novelist) and Grandma Moses (a woman who started painting when she was in her seventies and became a legendary folk artist) show us that we always have the opportunity for greatness.

Deep down, we believe that you never have to be stuck in what you do. Self-reinvention is definitely on Code. If your work no longer provides you with the sense of who you are that you desire, it is not only acceptable but also preferable to seek something new. Americans champion entrepreneurs because they are our most aggressive identity-seekers. They don't wait for someone to tell them what to be, but rather take significant risks to become what they believe they should be.

Entrepreneurs are inspirational to us because they set their own course for identity evolution. We all want to believe that we are headed somewhere in our work, that we aren't going to stay in the same place for the rest of our lives. Most of us have an ideal job in mind, and it usually involves movement of some sort from our current place (bigger office, bigger staff, being the boss, being able to quit that second job). Since work suggests who we are to us, we put significant stock into this progression. None of us want to feel that we are "done," that who we are will remain stagnant for the remainder of our lives. Retirees, after decades of work, seek new jobs in retirement, even when money isn't an object. We saw earlier that they do so in part because they dread immobility, which is equivalent to death. It is significant, though, that the activity they choose is work. They don't work because they need the income; they work because they so strongly connect their identities with the work they do that they feel the need to keep working in order to feel that they still exist.

So what does one do with knowledge of the Code? From an employer's perspective, the Code offers a path to making the most of employee relations, as Ritz-Carlton has. The understanding that employees connect their jobs with who they are makes it clear that employers should put a premium on keeping staff inspired. Calling regular staff meetings to solicit input on how to improve a company is on Code. Involving staff in the direction of the company gives them an elevated sense of identity, the feeling that they are integral to the company's success.

Similarly, helping employees understand their career paths is on Code. If someone can see that a clerical position leads to a position with greater responsibility, which leads to a management position, a middle management position, and ultimately an executive position, she can see that she is going somewhere, and that heightens her sense of who she is.

Employees always expect monetary rewards to accompany promotions, but an on-Code employer takes rewards further. Promotions should come with new responsibilities and especially with new tools to help the employee do a more effective job (a better computer, access to an expense account, operation of machinery that is more powerful). In addition to giving him a way to do his job better, such changes give him a visceral sense that his identity is expanding.

One of the common mistakes that employers make is looking at a team of employees (for instance a sales force or a marketing staff) as a homogenous group that rises and falls together. Offering incentives (a group bonus or a vacation trip) to a team as a whole is off Code because it fails to acknowledge who an individual is. While teamwork is important within a corporation, the team should be regarded as a support group that allows individuals to become champions. Think of a jazz band. The band lays down a basic musical structure that allows each soloist to shine. When a saxophonist plays a stirring solo, he receives individual recognition (applause after the solo) above the other members of the band (who will get the chance for recognition during their own solos later in the song). Sending an entire team to the Bahamas for a job well done actually blunts an employee's efforts to do his best work. He only needs to perform well enough to help achieve the team objective. If, on the other hand, the employee knew that individual rewards were possible, he would be more likely to strive to outperform expectations.

"SHOW ME THE MONEY"

Ask most people why they work and they're likely to answer "To make money." The Culture Code shows us that this isn't actually true, but there *is* a very strong connection between work and money in this culture.

The Code for money offers a very powerful tool for understanding America. People around the world perceive us as being concerned only with money. This huge misconception is one of the reasons so many of them fail to see what really does motivate us. At the same time, though, Americans themselves perceive this preoccupation with money and think it suggests that we are greedy at heart or that we prize material goods over enhancement of the spirit. This, too, is a misconception, one that gives us much less credit than we deserve.

There is very little "old money" in America. The overwhelming preponderance of the wealth in this country belongs to the person who originally earned it. Our culture is filled with "self-made" people, and in some very real way, we all have the same starting point with regard to wealth—we all began poor. We came here with no money and established the goal of making life better for our children. Some succeeded in extraordinary ways immediately, while others simply improved the situation slightly for the next generation. Regardless, the notion that we "come from nothing" pervades America. In a sense, we have the poorest rich people in the world, because even those who accumulate huge sums of money think like poor people. They continue to work hard, they continue to focus on cash flow and expenses, and they continue to struggle to earn more.

A discovery undertaken for J. P. Morgan and Citibank revealed why. Listen to the third-hour stories:

I still have the first dollar I received when I opened the doors at my dry-cleaning business. It's in a frame in my office in the back of the store. I look at it every morning to remind me that my business is a good one.—*a sixty-two-year-old man*

My dad got injured one spring when I was a teenager, so he asked me to turn over the vegetable garden for him and put in new plants. This was much harder work than anything I ever did before and there were a couple of times when I thought about quitting. I kept going, though, because I knew my father needed me to do it. When I finished, he gave me twenty bucks, which was a decent amount of cash at the time. I wound up getting a radio I really wanted with it. I held on to that radio for a long time because I worked so hard to get it.—*a man in his fifties*

My first, most powerful, and most recent memory of money is that I don't have any. Whatever I make goes to pay the bills. I never expected it to be like this after all these years. I don't know how I'll ever get out of this hole.—*a forty-three-year-old man*

We never had money when I was growing up and I had to take out a lot of loans to pay for college. That felt like a huge burden when I graduated. Fortunately, I got a good job right away and after some quick promotions, I was making good money. One of the first things I did was pay off my student loans. I loved that I could do that and still have plenty of money left over.—*a thirty-two-year-old woman*

My most powerful memory is going in and asking my boss for a raise for the first time. I was doing okay and I didn't need the money all that much, but I also knew I was making a lot of money for him and that I deserved it. He gave me a hard time at first, but then he gave in. It felt great to know that he appreciated me enough to pay me more.—*a thirty-five-year-old man*

I was the fifth of five kids in my family, and all of my siblings were significantly older than me. Whenever we went out together, one of them always paid my way, which was necessary because I didn't have much money, but always made me feel a little bad. One night—this is my most powerful memory—we all went out to dinner at an Italian restaurant. The food was great and we all had a really good time. When the check came, I reached across the table and grabbed it. They tried to argue with me, but I told them I'd just gotten a little bonus at work and wanted to treat everyone. They were very proud of me and I felt like I had a different place in the family after that.—*a woman in her thirties*

This whole session has been difficult for me. I try not to think too much about money. I'm up to my neck in bills and I don't have a clue how I'm going to pay them off. Most of my friends have more money than I do and I try to fake it and keep up with them when we're out. I know I can't keep up, though, and it's gonna kill me if I don't stop.—*a twenty-four-year-old man*

Clearly, money signifies more to Americans than the means to buy things. It shows us how we're doing, tells us how far we've come from impoverished poor roots. Money reminds you that your "business is a good one," that you've worked hard to get something, that you can carry your burdens, that you are appreciated, and that you are moving up to the next level. Not having money makes you feel as if you are "in a hole"; you may feel that "it's gonna kill me."

The American culture has no titles of nobility to show us who the big winners are. Without them, we need something that performs a similar function. Participants tell us through their third-hour stories that that thing is money.

The American Culture Code for money is PROOF.

In spite of what people from other cultures—and many from our own—say about our attitude toward money, the Code shows that money isn't a goal in and of itself for most Americans. We rely on it to show us that we are good, that we have true value in the world. An American can't be knighted for his deeds or become a baroness, as Margaret Thatcher has. American accolades are relative and ephemeral. We can prove what we've accomplished only by making as much money as possible.

Money is our barometer of success. Most Americans find it impossible to feel successful if they feel they are underpaid. Money is a scorecard. If someone is doing a job similar to yours and making more money, you unconsciously believe that he or she is doing a better job. Being paid for a job imbues it with instant credibility. I spoke with someone recently who told me about his early struggles to become a professional writer after leaving a corporate career. For two years, even though he was doing high-quality work, he failed to make any money at it. "I felt unemployed," he told me, "even though I was working ten hours a day." A publishing contract changed his attitude about his accomplishments instantly. Suddenly the previous two years gained validity. The money the publisher paid him was proof.

Because we believe money is proof, we see a very strong connection between money and work. Money earned via hard work is admirable, proof that you are a good person. We have little respect, however, for those who inherit money rather than making it on their own. We might be fascinated by the exploits of someone like Paris Hilton, but we don't feel that she's proven anything, because she was born rich and her celebrity stems exclusively from her wealth. We attribute Patty Hearst's early difficulties to her growing up an heiress, and we consider the ongoing problems of the Getty children to be the product of old money. We love it that Bill Gates has more money than the Queen of England, because he earned every penny of it himself.

While we don't have much respect for trust fund babies who live off the family fortune, we have completely different feelings about those who build on their inherited legacy and establish substantial careers of their own. Robert Wood Johnson worked hard to take Johnson & Johnson to new levels of growth and profitability. William Clay Ford Jr. did the same with the Ford Motor Company. These people, while starting from a very different place from most Americans, prove themselves by making their own money and increasing the family fortune. Wealthy American businesspeople will say that they want their children to establish themselves. They will of course provide access and connections (and they might underestimate the extent to which this makes a difference), but they won't give their children a "free ride." Making every generation prove itself anew is definitely on Code.

Even if we work very hard, we can find this good money/bad money dichotomy in our own lives. One of the things revealed by the study I did for Morgan and Citibank is that Americans see interest income and capital gains as "bad money" because they didn't earn it themselves. Investors who took a very active role in managing their stock portfolios felt they "made" this money, while those who simply followed the advice of their brokers did not. Banks and investment firms that tell their customers "Give us your money, and we'll make it work for you" are totally off Code. On-Code firms portray themselves as facilitators who provide their clients with tools for generating more money.

Many European cultures have a different view of money and its function. At a certain point, if one earns a great deal of money in these cultures, one simply settles back on the estate, leaving the world of commerce behind. Here, of course, we believe we're only as good as our last deal, and even when we've made billions we want to make billions more to prove how good we are. In America, we can dream about having no limits, about striking it rich regardless of how little we had at birth. In Europe, you might start out with a bit of money, but it is considerably more difficult to grow out of your station (a French book published a few years ago whose title can be translated as "The Heirs" showed that there was very little economic movement in that country: the children of doctors became doctors, the children of bankers became bankers, and it was very difficult to move into these classes or beyond them). Hence, money in France isn't a form of proof, but an unpleasant fact.

In France, a common topic at elegant dinner parties is sex. The French consider it entirely acceptable to discuss sexual positions, multiple partners, and different kinds of lingerie while entertaining guests. They consider the topic of money, however, to be vulgar; it is exceedingly impolite to ask how much money someone makes or how much he or she paid for something. Here, of course, we would be appalled by an explicit sexual discussion at dinner, but we can talk about money all night long. Different Culture Codes lead to different behaviors.

It has been said that Americans consider money their religion. While this is often meant critically, it has an element of truth that doesn't have a negative dimension. The "proof" that we derive from money is the proof of our goodness—not only of the quality of our work at our chosen professions, but also of our quality as people. We truly believe there is a link between goodness and monetary success and that those who cheat and lie their way to the top ultimately meet their comeuppance on both the spiritual and financial planes. Consistent with this mind-set is the American attitude toward charitable donations. There is no luggage rack on a hearse, and since you cannot take your possessions and money into the afterlife with you, Americans (not just dying ones) choose to give a significant amount of it away to those in need. Studies show that Americans are the most charitable people in the world. Even people who barely scrape by tend to be generous with the money they share with others. The rich even appear to compete over who makes the largest donations. While the generosity seems to be heartfelt, there is a strong sense of obligation that comes with being wealthy in this culture. Americans expect their most fortunate to share what they've earned, and we have an entire system of laws in place for giving one's money away.

The new glasses of the Culture Code offer us strong, even counterintuitive, insights into dealing with money in America. It is off Code, for example, to preach profitability to one's employees. Money is the proof of goodness, not in itself the goal. Instead, a company's management must inspire employees to be the best they can possibly be and to make the company as strong as it can possibly be. This is on Code for both work and money and, if done effectively, leads to profitability.

The two Codes together lead to another surprising conclusion: money alone is the worst reward for an American employee. It doesn't last and it is never sufficient. Yes, money is proof, and as such, it is a critical component of any reward system. But the most on-Code approach is to use money as a global positioning system that shows the employee where he is on his career path. At every promotion, the employee should be shown a visual representation of the income curve that he or she is on. The angle at which one's salary is climbing is a powerful symbol of growth. It is visual proof. A tangible award of some sort presented at the same time as the promotion gives the employee a tactile experience of his enhanced sense of who he is. Maybe it is a plaque of some sort. Maybe it is a new office, or a new accessory for the office. These tangible symbols last much longer than money, though they admittedly mean very little without it.

WORK AND MONEY: AN AMERICAN MARRIAGE BUILT TO LAST

The Codes show that Americans draw a very strong connection between work and money. The sense of "who you are" derived from work is intertwined with the "proof" provided by the money one earns. We are suspicious, and even dismissive, of money gained without hard work. For instance, we have little respect for those who gain sudden wealth through the lottery. Americans don't regard this as "real" money because it isn't earned. A lottery winner *proves* nothing by winning the lottery, except that he or she was very fortunate. Lottery winners themselves seem to share some of this sensibility. Their instant wealth makes them anomalies: they don't truly belong with the rich, because they didn't work their way into that world, nor do they fit any longer among their peers, because their money separates them. We tend to forget the names of lottery winners within a day or so and never hear from them again.

Interestingly, we look at game show winners differently. Of course, this is on Code. When Ken Jennings won seventy-four consecutive rounds of the quiz show *Jeopardy!* (acquiring more than $2.5 million in the process), he became an instant celebrity. Unlike a lottery winner's, however, Jennings's star didn't fade immediately. He received endorsement deals, speaking engagements, and a place in television history. Ken Jennings earned his money by battling and beating contestants for months; he *proved* himself repeatedly.

THE CULTURE CODE   129

Ken Jennings received an opportunity and he made the most of it. This is what we really want as Americans. We may dream of winning the lottery and escaping the rat race. What the Codes for work and money show, though, is that work is an essential part of who we are and that we just want a chance to prove ourselves and receive tangible evidence that we have succeeded.

Chapter 7

LEARNING TO LIVE WITH IT

The Codes for Quality and Perfection

A s we've established, a culture is a survival kit we inherit at birth. Our culture is what it is (and it changes very, very slowly) because it is best suited to the conditions under which its members live. Because of this, attempts to impose changes that are fundamentally opposed to the Code of a particular culture are destined to fail. Our attempts in the late 1980s and early 1990s to adopt a Japanese business model for quality are an excellent illustration of this point. Their failure offers important lessons for how we do business today.

During this period, there was an economic slump in the United States, while the Japanese economy was growing robustly; many American companies questioned why the Japanese were succeeding while they floundered. Many believed the answer was quality. The strict Japanese commitment to zero defects and constant improvement led to their primacy in automobiles, computers, home electronics, appliances, and many other major consumer goods. Their products were cheaper *and* better, a nearly unbeatable combination. American consumers bought Japanese goods at unprecedented levels, boosting the Japanese economy and hindering ours. Many U.S. companies concluded that if they were to compete against the Japanese for the *American* dollar (let alone to compete on the world stage), they must adopt the Japanese approach to quality.

This foray failed. Our quality standards are not appreciably better today than they were in the 1980s, though corporations spent billions of dollars trying to change this. Why? The answer lies in the Codes.

PLUG AND PLAY—THAT'S ENOUGH

In the late 1980s, AT&T commissioned me to discover the Code for quality in America. Like many huge American companies, AT&T felt the Japanese had mastered quality and was vexed at our inability to keep pace. The company used the Code to train fifty thousand managers, shared the results with the American Quality Foundation, and developed it into a book, *Incredibly American,* by Marilyn R. Zuckerman and Lewis J. Hatala.*

As always, the Code itself was revealed by the stories people told during our discovery sessions:

> My first memory of quality was the first remote control television we got when I was a kid. You had to sit in a specific part of the room to make the remote work, but it was so impressive to me that you didn't have to get up to change the channels anymore. —*a man in his forties*

> The first time I remember being aware of quality was when the buzzer on my "Operation" game stopped working. I went crying to my mother and she tried to console me by telling me that things just stop working after a while and that I couldn't expect a game like that to last. That wasn't very consoling, actually, but these years later, I know what she means.—*a thirty-nine-year-old man*

*Milwaukee: ASQ Quality Press, 1992.

I had this great clock radio when I was growing up. The reception went in and out, but the alarm always worked. I never missed a day of school from oversleeping with that thing . . . which, now that I think about it, probably wasn't a good thing. Maybe I should have talked my mother into getting me a clock radio that didn't work so well.—*a thirty-six-year-old woman*

I don't have any powerful memories of quality. I have powerful memories of *lack* of quality, though. Like the laptop my parents bought me for my eighteenth birthday. That monster has crashed and wiped out college papers on me more times than I care to remember—and I have to restart it three times every time I use it. I don't want to complain about it to my parents because I know it cost them a lot of money, but it definitely doesn't do its job.—*a nineteen-year-old woman*

My '64 Ford Impala was a quality car. That thing was indestructible! Not exactly a luxury automobile, and I don't even want to think about the gas mileage (which didn't matter much at the time), but I'll bet someone is still driving that baby around. —*a fifty-two-year-old man*

I'll tell you something that isn't quality—the new thousand-dollar dishwasher my wife convinced me to buy. It breaks down every other day. We've already had a repairman at the house three times. If it wasn't under warranty, I'd throw that piece of garbage in the trash heap.—*a fifty-four-year-old man*

My mother was quality. I know that probably isn't what you meant by the question, but that's my most powerful memory. No matter how she was feeling, no matter how sick she might be, she was always there for us. I've never had a better example of quality in my life.—*a sixty-one-year-old woman*

It became clear that Americans imprinted the notion of quality in a very different way from the Japanese. In fact, the very first imprint of quality for many of us is a negative one. It comes when something doesn't do what it is supposed to do. The child's game quits; the computer crashes; the dishwasher turns the repairman into a family member. Our positive imprints regarding quality focus on functionality rather than the brilliance of the design or the excellence of its performance. The remote control requires one to be in a specific place, but at least it changes the channels. The clock radio isn't much of a radio, but it's a reliable clock. The car doesn't have luxurious amenities, but it keeps on moving.

These stories and the hundreds of similar ones told over the course of the study showed that quality means something different to Americans than it does to the Japanese, something less exalted.

The Culture Code for quality in America is IT WORKS.

This standard falls quite a bit short of "zero defects." Indeed, it invited the question "If quality means merely functionality, then what does perfection mean?" During the discovery sessions for perfection, the messages in the stories were equally declarative:

I have no memories of perfection. Does anyone? To me, perfection is not a part of this life.—*a fifty-seven-year-old woman*

The one perfect thing in my life is my six-year-old daughter. I can't imagine thinking anything else was perfect. Perfection just isn't reality.—*a thirty-seven-year-old woman*

Everything I ever thought was perfect ultimately lets me down— products, people, it's all the same. Maybe things are perfect in some other universe, but definitely not in this one.—*a forty-eight-year-old man*

I've never encountered anything perfect in my life. I'm not even sure that I'd want to. If something was perfect then nothing could ever get any better. I don't like that idea.—*a twenty-six-year-old woman*

A buddy of mine bowled a perfect game one night. We bought him beers and had a huge celebration. It was very exciting. The next time we went bowling, he bowled a 143 or something like that—just awful. It made me wonder just how perfect a perfect game was if it went away so quickly.—*a fifty-five-year-old man*

Phrases like "not a part of this life," "just isn't reality," and "definitely not in this [universe]" characterized perfection as something abstract and inchoate, something distant and maybe even undesirable. In fact, the quest for perfection seemed to be something most people preferred to avoid, something that defined the end of a process, after which there could be no further movement.

The Culture Code for perfection in America is DEATH.

Knowledge of the Codes for quality and perfection helps explain why our attempts at Japanese-level standards in these areas failed to gain traction. Americans understand the concept of "getting it right the first time" at the cortex level, but deeper down they don't want to do it, might even fear doing it. The cultural reasons for this seem to be twofold. Partly it's because we are an adolescent culture with an adolescent attitude. We don't want people telling us what to do and holding us to their standards. We want to discover things and learn how to do things our own way. Even more entrenched, though, is the pioneer spirit that brought us to this country in the first place. When we arrived in the New World, there was no instruction manual teaching us how to deal with the conditions. We had to learn everything ourselves, and we did it the only way we could—through trial and error. Learning from our mistakes not only allowed us to survive, but also helped us to grow into a powerful and hugely successful country. We were rewarded for our ability to pick ourselves up off the ground and do things better the *second* and *third* times.

Trying, failing, learning from our mistakes, and coming back stronger than ever is an essential part of the American archetype. We fluctuate between periods when we are Superman (as we were during and after World War II) and periods when we are a Sleeping Giant (as we were in the late 1980s and early 1990s, before the Internet revolution). How many times have European "experts" predicted the demise of America? Whenever America "falls asleep" (in the late 1970s, for instance), these people delight in saying that America has become irrelevant. This demonstrates a fundamental misunderstanding of the American culture. Failure and fallow periods are part of what makes America what it is, and we always come back stronger and in a more dominant position. The path of American progress is filled with high peaks and low valleys, but the peaks always get higher. Recently, the billionaire investor Kirk Kerkorian bought a huge number of shares in General Motors. Given the firm's flagging performance, this seems counterintuitive. Kerkorian is betting that GM is in fact a sleeping giant, which will not only solve its problems but also solve them in a way that returns it to market leadership. He's betting on the cycle and, given his investment history, there's every reason to believe he knows what he's doing. If you look at the headlines and at world opinion today, you might say that our culture overall is in something of a valley; our economy is flat, our foreign policy is stumbling, many government institutions fail to provide essential services. Anyone who believes this valley is an indication of permanent decline hasn't been paying attention to the larger pattern.

Because our country was so vast and underpopulated when we de-

veloped it, we have grown accustomed to a certain level of disposabil-
ity. If the land we farmed didn't produce enough, we got new land. If
the environment in one part of the country proved inhospitable, we
moved. There was no need to improve the quality of one's house, because it was easier simply to get a new and better house.

This is fundamentally different from the way many other cultures
learned to survive. Take, for instance, the Japanese. Their country
comprises only 146,000 square miles (compared to the more than 3.7
million square miles of the United States). There was never a vast
frontier to explore. The Japanese couldn't "dispose" of their houses
or their property if they grew disenchanted; they needed to make the
most of their land and to keep it as productive as possible. In addition, because so many people live in such a small space (the population of Japan is more than 125 million; that's 43 percent of the
American population in 4 percent of the space), efficiency is critical.
There's no room for wasted products or wasted process. Mistakes are
costlier. Quality is a necessity. Perfection is premium.

Americans, on the other hand, find perfection boring. If something is perfect, you're stuck with it for life, and that doesn't sit
well with most Americans. We want a new car every three years.
We want a new television every five. We want a new house when
we have kids, and another new one when the kids grow up. My
fourteen-year-old son, born and raised in this country, exemplifies this
attitude. I went shopping for antiques recently and took him with
me. We came upon a gorgeous seventeenth-century sofa and I told
him how much I liked it. "You like that?" he said, sneering. "Do you
know how many asses have sat in that sofa? Why don't you get a *new*
sofa?"

The "perfect" car would be useless to us, because we wouldn't
have the alibi that our old car doesn't work well enough anymore and
we need to change it. On the cortex level, we scorn planned obsolescence (the practice many manufacturers employ of building some-

thing that needs to be replaced within a relatively short period), but planned obsolescence is on Code with the American culture. We want things to become obsolete, because when they do we have the excuse we need to buy something new.

At the same time, though, we have a simple and clear quality demand for our products: they need to work. When we turn the keys in the ignitions of our cars, we expect them to start and to take us where we need to go. When we make a call on our cell phones, we expect to get through and are frustrated when the cell network suddenly drops our call. None of our products needs to perform brilliantly (our cars don't need to be masterpieces of engineering, our cell phones don't need to provide sonic perfection), but they absolutely need to *perform*. Other cultures might have higher standards for performance or design, but we insist on something simpler: make sure the thing operates the way it was supposed to. Thus the Verizon cell phone campaign "Can you hear me now?"

This ties directly into another fundamental component of our culture. Remember, the Code for health in America is movement. We are a nation of doers. Life, in essence, is movement. When a product works—when it either helps us to keep moving or doesn't prevent us from moving (the car takes us to our destination, the cell phone connects)—it is on Code. When it fails to work—when it gets in the way of our ability to move (the car spends too much time in the shop, the cell phone cuts off for no reason)—it is off Code.

The cup holder in a car, for instance, is absolutely on Code. What a brilliant notion: a simple device that lets us take our coffee with us. Ten minutes less spent drinking coffee at home means ten minutes more out in the world doing what we need to do. Volkswagen recently introduced an air-cooled glove compartment for its Jetta. Again, this is dead-on. Now we can stick our lunch in the glove compartment and just keep moving.

So what does this mean for a company selling goods and services in America? The most important message is that Americans put a premium on functionality. We are not a bells-and-whistles culture. We would far rather have a cell phone that always operates when we're in the middle of a call than one that takes pictures, plays music, and allows us to download television clips. A car that reliably gets us to work, the supermarket, or soccer practice is much more valuable to us than one that corners masterfully or has rain-sensing windshield wipers.

BlackBerry offers an on-Code example of functionality with its PDAs. The BlackBerry market consists of on-the-go executives, people who spend a great deal of time on the road, in airports, and in others' offices. Remote e-mail access is a business essential to these executives, but accessing e-mail remotely can be a chore if you have to spend long minutes logging on to a server and waiting for a wireless link. BlackBerry addresses this by notifying users when they have e-mail (one of the company's slogans is "You don't check your e-mail—it checks you"), making it necessary to log on only when you know something is waiting.

Because we equate perfection with death, we don't expect anyone to make the perfect product. We expect our products to break down. However, because our Code for quality is IT WORKS, we expect problems to be resolved quickly and with a minimum of disruption. Americans are far more responsive to good service than they are to perfection (which they don't believe in, anyway). Crisis is a great opportunity to create loyalty. If a customer comes to you with a problem with a product or service and you solve that problem quickly and minimize the customer's inconvenience, you will likely earn that customer's dedication. You have proven yourself to the customer.

Ironically, if your product never breaks down, you never have the opportunity to develop this relationship with the customer. When the customer seeks to replace the product (as he inevitably will), he is likely to look elsewhere, because he hasn't formed a bond with you.

The bottom line is that great service is more important to Americans than great quality.

A colleague of mine recently purchased a Compaq computer. His previous machine, from another manufacturer, worked adequately, but Compaq offered him more computer for his money. Within weeks, the computer exhibited serious performance problems. Perturbed, my colleague called the Compaq tech support line, expecting to wait hours for human help. Instead, within five minutes, a tech support person was guiding him through a series of diagnostics and getting to the core of the problem. He was impressed with this service and happy to get his computer purring once again. A few hours later, however, he was stunned to receive a follow-up call from the same tech support person asking whether everything was okay with his computer and whether he had any further questions. By the time he hung up, he'd become an unofficial spokesperson for Compaq.

Hyundai, the Korean car manufacturer, seems to understand how the promise of great service can dramatically improve the value of something of only modest quality. The challenge for Hyundai was to introduce a new brand—from a country with no proven success in the American market—into the intensely competitive low-end category. Hyundai's sales foundered until they introduced a ten-year bumper-to-bumper warranty on their cars, including roadside assistance and loaner cars. The message seemed to be "Yes, we know there isn't much to this car, but we'll keep you on the road." That was on Code and it connected with the American public. Hyundai's sales have risen dramatically since.

NOT TURNING JAPANESE

Major American corporations spent huge sums of money in the late 1980s and early 1990s trying to make their quality standards match those of the Japanese. At the cortex level, this makes perfect sense.

Higher quality should generate better business. In the end, though, this movement failed. You no longer hear American companies stressing zero defects or continuous improvement. Why? Because it is out of sync with the American culture, and nothing that contradicts the Code of a culture succeeds for any length of time. Americans don't put a premium on quality. We just want something that works. We don't believe in perfection, so the concept of zero defects seems like a fantasy. Notions that are a necessary part of the Japanese survival kit are completely off Code here. We therefore rejected them.

We would respond the same way to any other concept incompatible with our culture. Remember how Nestlé tried to convince the Japanese to give up tea for coffee, and how unsuccessful they were? That they even tried seems silly to us now. When one seeks to bring something new to a culture, one must adapt the idea to the culture. It doesn't work the other way.

Chapter 8

MORE IS MORE

The Codes for Food and Alcohol

O ne of the things that intrigued me when I first came to this country was the all-you-can-eat buffet. We didn't have such a thing in France; in fact, I'd never seen one anywhere in Europe. Yet in America, in every town I visited, I saw signs hanging in numerous restaurants announcing "All you can eat: $9.99 (the price was lower in the 1970s, but you get the point). I found this baffling. My experience with American restaurants was that they always served me *more* than I could eat. Why, then, make a marketing point of serving *all* you could eat? Even more confounding was what I discovered when I visited one of these buffets: people loading up their plates with absurd amounts of various kinds of food and eating it as quickly as they could so they could get back to the buffet.

Why does a $9.99 all-you-can-eat buffet cause a literal feeding frenzy?

Why is fast food an American institution that will never die?

Why is "going out to get drunk" a common social behavior here and extremely unusual in Europe?

As ever, the answers are in the Codes.

FILLING UP THE TANK

Dining in America is an entirely different experience from what it is in France. Here, we want our food as quickly as we can get it, even in a fine restaurant. The French, on the other hand, invented the notion of slow food. Even if they can make a dish quickly, they won't, because they believe it is important first to set the mood for the diner and to build anticipation of the upcoming meal. In America, we put several different kinds of food—meat, fish, vegetables, starches, sometimes even fruit and cheese—on one plate because that is the most efficient way to serve a meal. In France, each kind of food comes on a different plate, to keep the flavors from mixing and to allow the diner to enjoy the separate qualities of each preparation. Americans want abundant quantities of all food and it is our goal to finish everything served to us. French portions are significantly smaller, and the French consider you vulgar if your plate or wineglass is empty at the conclusion of dinner. Americans end a meal by saying "I'm full." The French end a meal by saying "That was delicious."

You can trace many of the American traits to our humble beginnings. Though we are the richest country in the world, as we discussed earlier, at the reptilian level we consider ourselves poor. We start out with nothing and we labor to achieve wealth, and even though we may succeed, the hand-to-mouth attitude remains. The response of poor people to food is consistent throughout the world: they eat as much as they can when they can, because they don't know whether they will have the opportunity to eat the next day. This attitude is similar to that of many predators: when they capture any prey, they eat as much as possible because they can't be certain of capturing more prey tomorrow. In this spirit, we eat all of the food available to us and only then do we feel satisfied. When someone eats huge quantities, we sometimes say he "can really put it away." Unconsciously, this is exactly what he is doing. He is storing as much food as he can to forestall starvation (though the chances of starvation are extremely slim).

This is a situation in which our modest beginnings and our quest for abundance intersect. At the reptilian level, uncertainty about tomorrow's meal tells us to eat lustily before the food goes away. While our cortexes tell us that the food will be available at the buffet all night, our reptilian brains aren't taking any chances. In this battle between the brains, as in all such battles, the reptilian wins.

Though other cultures have certainly had their share of hunger and even starvation, many have other influences that moderate the desire to "put it away." The Italian culture, for instance, is strongly influenced by the model of aristocracy. An aristocrat would never gorge himself at a buffet. An aristocrat would never rush through his meal. An aristocrat tastes each morsel and appreciates the flavor and consistency. This aristocratic approach to food has trickled down to every level of Italian society. Regardless of their station, Italians have a strong sense of refinement when it comes to food and believe that overeating destroys their ability to appreciate taste. It is extremely unusual to find a buffet at any price in Italy.

At the limbic level, Americans strongly connect food with love. Obviously, this comes from our earliest memories of being fed by our mothers. Feeding is associated with being held, cuddled, and made to feel safe. As we get older, though our mothers no longer feed us in the same way (though they continue to ask us, as soon as they see us, whether we want anything to eat), the intense feeling of satisfaction that comes with food remains. In America, food is "safe sex." Whereas we unconsciously have negative feelings about sex, we find it universally acceptable to take food into our bodies for pleasure. Perhaps that it why so many of us eat so often and to such extremes.

The pleasure we derive from eating, however, pales next to our need for movement, our desire to fill our time with activity. We are a country on the go and we don't have time to linger over our food. It was recently reported that the average American spends *six minutes* eating dinner. Dallying is for laggards like the French. Eating on the run is a national pastime, and many of us regularly gobble meals (often purchased from a fast-food restaurant) in our cars (keeping the drinks in our cup holders, of course) on the way to our next appointment. There's nothing either safe or sexy about that experience.

Consider these observations—that we regard food in a different way from the Europeans, that we eat as though we were still poor, that food is "safe sex," and that we think of eating as an act requiring efficiency—as you read these third-hour stories:

I try to make a nice dinner for my family at least twice a week, but we don't sit down together all that often. The rest of the time, we're eating on the fly—on the way to practices, lessons, clubs, and late nights at the office. I try to keep things in the house that will provide good nutrition to the kids and that they can fill up with quickly.—*a forty-one-year-old woman*

My most recent memory of food is this deli I found near one of my accounts. They make these huge hero sandwiches that I can eat while I'm going to my next appointment. They taste good and they really keep me going.—*a fifty-year-old man*

I'm a health nut and I'm really particular about the food I eat. I limit the fat and carbs I take in and I only eat lean meats and organic vegetables. To me, there's no point in eating if the food doesn't help keep you healthy. I plan to live a long time. —*a twenty-seven-year-old woman*

I like pasta, but it always makes me sleepy. I figured out a while ago that if I had anything other than protein during lunch, I wasn't as good in the afternoon. When the Atkins diet came along, I thought it was the best thing in the world. Bacon cheese-burgers for lunch every day—and I actually had more energy. —*a thirty-four-year-old man*

My first memory of food was the first time my father took me to a McDonald's. I swear I got a buzz off the fries. Now that I'm on my own, I go there as often as I can for those fries. I know some people say they're bad for you, but they make me feel great. I heard there was a guy who made a movie about going on an all-McDonald's diet. I could definitely do that.—*a twenty-two-year-old man*

I have the memory of some great meals, but to be honest with you, most of them have more to do with the people I was with than the food I ate. I can't tell you what I ate at most of the fancy restaurants I've been to, but I can tell you what we talked about. Eating was never that important to me. Sometimes people have to remind me to eat and I really only do it to keep going. —*a thirty-three-year-old woman*

Not all the stories read this way, of course. America has a subculture of food aficionados, "foodies," who admire food and take pleasure in its masterful preparation. We have a twenty-four-hour cable television network devoted to food, dozens of food magazines are published monthly, and there are fine restaurants (some of the finest in the world) all over the country. Yet the responses of the vast majority of participants in the discovery suggest that the foodie subculture, vibrant though it might be, is not representative of the way most Americans feel about food.

The overwhelming majority of responses I received spoke not of the pleasures of the palate, but rather of the *function* of food. "Good nutrition that they can fill up with quickly." "Bacon cheeseburgers for lunch every day—and I actually had more energy." "There's no point in eating if the food doesn't keep you healthy." "I really only do it to keep going." For every gourmet who spoke about taste, texture, and savoring a meal, there were two dozen people who talked about filling up and eating as a necessity instead of a pleasure. The message that came through loudly from these stories was that the body is a machine and the job of food is to keep the machine running.

The American Culture Code for food is FUEL.

Americans say "I'm full" at the end of a meal because unconsciously they think of eating as refueling. Their mission has been to fill up their tanks; when they complete it, they announce that they've finished the task. It is also interesting to note that on highways all across the country, you will find rest stops that combine gas stations and food courts. When you drive up to the pump and tell the attendant to fill up your tank, it wouldn't be entirely inappropriate for him to ask "Which one?"

Americans regard their bodies as machines. Our machines have functions to perform and we need to keep them working. Some of us choose to keep our machines in top shape by attaching them to other machines—the workout equipment at our local health club, which appears to have been designed by the Marquis de Sade. All of us know, though, that we need fuel to run these machines.

Interestingly, we seem far less concerned with the quality of the fuel than one might expect. In spite of abundant warnings about health effects, Americans love fast food. In his book *Fast Food Nation,* Eric Schlosser notes that "Americans now spend more money on fast food than they do on higher education, personal computers, software, or new cars. They spend more on fast food than on movies, books, magazines, newspapers, videos, and recorded music—combined. In 1970, Americans spent about $6 billion on fast food. Last year they spent more than $100 billion."

Regardless of how one feels about its taste or nutritional quality, fast food is definitely on Code. Fast-food restaurants provide us with a quick fill-up. We don't need to wait for our meals and, refueled, we can go on to our other tasks. This appeals to our need for movement as well as our adolescent desire to have everything now. One might argue that fast food isn't particularly good fuel to put in one's tank, but then again, how many of us put regular gas in our cars even when the manufacturer tells us to use premium?

In many other cultures, food isn't a tool, but rather a means of experiencing refinement. In France, the purpose of food is pleasure, and even a home-cooked meal is something diners savor for a long period. In French restaurants, the meal is symphonic in its artistry, with many "performers"—the chef, the waiter, the sommelier, and the maître d'—working synchronously. In fact, the French use the word *chef* for both a fine cook and the conductor of an orchestra.

In Japan, the preparation and the enjoyment of food are a means to approach perfection. Sushi chefs rigorously study the art of the knife, knowing that a perfectly cut piece of fish offers superior taste and texture. The Japanese consider the best sushi chefs to be masters—artists of the highest degree.

As we've already discussed, going against the Codes of a culture is a futile exercise. Therefore, it is unrealistic to believe that a large percentage of Americans will ever perceive food as pleasure or perfection rather than as fuel. What does this mean for the food industry?

Selling quantity before quality makes sense. The all-you-can-eat buffet hits all the right notes: it provides plenty of food that is available immediately. Restaurants that emphasize large portion size are likely to find a continuous stream of customers. Americans expect huge portions (portions astonishing to foreigners) even in the finest restaurants. You might recall the early days of nouvelle cuisine when American restaurateurs served small portions with elaborate presentation. The American market failed to embrace the trend, because it was off Code. Today, serving sizes even in most high-end establishments are gigantic, leading to the incongruous sight of diners leaving four-star restaurants with doggie bags.

Selling speed, of course, makes tremendous sense. Supermarket shelves are filled with packaged foods that busy homemakers can microwave and have on the table in five minutes. Emphasizing a product's speed of preparation is right on Code because it connects with our need to eat on the go, to fill up the tank and get back to our missions.

Taco Bell recently launched a marketing campaign for its 99-cent menu in which various delighted patrons announce "I'm full!" This is obviously right on Code. They make it clear that one can fill up one's tank (and express great joy afterward) for very little money.

Red Bull, the energy-drink manufacturer, takes a different on-Code approach in marketing its product. Red Bull's advertising notes that the drink "gives you wings." The company's ads show cartoon characters drinking Red Bull and becoming charged with energy. The message here is that the drink is high-octane fuel that propels you through your busy life.

Some foods take an even more direct on-Code approach to market positioning. One can go to one's local supermarket and buy a Power-Bar to fill up with a potent amount of protein. There are nutritional supplements called Ultimate Diet Fuel, Yohimbe Fuel, and Blitz: Tim Brown's Body Fuel System. It's hard to be more on Code than that.

The Code suggests a huge opportunity for the food industry to further exploit the American perception of food as fuel that powers the body-machine. Given that we use our machines for different purposes at different times of day, and that different nutrients and vitamins help us perform certain tasks (B vitamins for energy, healthy fats for brain function, magnesium for relaxation, and so on), a food packager that sells its product as fuel for a specific kind of activity (for instance, a cereal that has one formula to get you started on your day, another that you could eat before sports practice, and a third that you could snack on before you do your homework) would be on Code in breakthrough fashion.

TWO CANS ARE BETTER THAN ONE

How and when one imprints an archetype affects the power and meaning of that archetype. The timing of the imprint of alcohol in our culture and the French culture offers an intriguing way to see this in action.

As mentioned earlier in the book, the French, while they don't allow their children to drink in quantity, will expose them to alcohol (specifically, wine) at a very early age, allowing them to take a sip or perhaps to dip a cookie in a glass of champagne. They teach their children that wine enhances food and that older, lower-alcohol wines are best because the alcohol inhibits the flavor of the wine.

Americans, with their strong history of temperance (this is one of the few Western cultures ever to make the consumption of alcohol illegal for all of its citizens), generally keep their children completely away from alcohol until they are well into their teens. Americans teach their children that alcohol is an intoxicant that can lead to irresponsible behavior.

Forbidden to drink alcohol as children, and learning little about it other than that it is "bad" for you, Americans end up imprinting alcohol at a rebellious age. When they gain access to alcohol (usually underage, which enhances the sense that they are doing something taboo), they know nothing of its pleasures, subtleties, or role as an enhancer of food, but they quickly discover its intoxicating qualities. Taste is unimportant. What matters is that this substance can do a job for you: it can get you drunk. As a bonus, your parents don't want you to do it, so you can rebel and get wasted at the same time.

Drunkenness is in no way unique to Americans. Yet the phrase "going out to get drunk" is quintessentially American. Certainly, people in most cultures seek inebriation in different forms, but only in America, with its incredibly strong work ethic and bias for action, is the mission stated so directly by so many. It seems to be the primary avocation of many American teenagers and college students—not going to a party, not going to a nightclub, not spending an evening with friends, but "going out to get drunk." American ingenuity has even devised the most efficient way to accomplish the task: a hat that allows us to suck two cans of beer through a straw at once.

So is the Code for alcohol similarly efficient—the equivalent of food as fuel, with the mission being inebriation? It is not nearly as straightforward as that. When Seagram, Jack Daniel's, and Gallo commissioned a discovery, the stories revealed first imprints that were anything but matter-of-fact.

My first memory of alcohol was when I was maybe seven or eight years old. My parents had some company over and I was bugging my father to give me a taste of his scotch. Eventually he said, "Sure, but you have to drink it down all at once." I did what he told me and I nearly choked to death. I also felt miserable for the rest of the day. I actually thought I was going to die.—*a forty-two-year-old man*

When I was thirteen, we sneaked into my friend's parents' liquor cabinet. None of us knew what we were doing, but we pulled out a bottle of vodka. My friend told me that she saw her parents drinking it with orange juice, so we mixed some up. We took our first taste and it tasted just like orange juice. So we put some more in—something like a quarter of the bottle. The sip I took after that tasted like bad medicine, but I felt the changes in my body almost instantly.—*a twenty-eight-year-old woman*

My most powerful memory was right after I started a new job. It was the boss's birthday and a bunch of us went out with him to celebrate. It turns out this was a huge event every year and that it all had to do with drinking. Everyone started doing shots in insane quantities. I was the new guy and I wanted to fit in, so I downed more than my share. I thought I was doing a good job of keeping up until I stood to go to the bathroom. I nearly collapsed right on the spot. I was sick for days after.—*a thirty-seven-year-old man*

I drank a lot in college. A lot. A whole lot. The thing I remember most about that time was that I always had a couple of quick drinks in my room alone before I went out to get me in the mood. Those drinks took me out of myself, which was definitely the idea in those days.—*a thirty-five-year-old woman*

Alcohol is a very powerful thing. It makes me feel strong. It helps me forget. It gives me added confidence. I could get by without it, but if I'm in a stressful situation, a couple of drinks are a nice thing to have on my side.—*a fifty-four-year-old man*

The study revealed that alcohol had a very powerful effect, with the ability to alter lives and change circumstances. The structure and imagery of the stories suggested something that could make you "feel miserable" and that you were "going to die," change your body almost instantly, cause you to "collapse right on the spot," take you "out of" yourself, and was "a nice thing to have on your side." Alcohol is more than fuel; it is something very powerful, instantaneous, and extreme.

The American Culture Code for alcohol is GUN.

This was a shocking and intense discovery. The American Code is in such sharp contrast to the European attitude toward alcohol. Yet perhaps it should not surprise us, given that there has always been a strong connection between alcohol and guns in this culture. Think of the Old West saloon and the recurring image of people getting drunk and getting into gunfights, or the sheriff taking a stiff drink of whiskey before facing down the villain in a duel. Think of the gangster subculture that emerged during Prohibition. Our word for a quick drink of hard liquor is "shot." No other culture uses this terminology. There's even a malt liquor on the market called Colt .45.

Hip-hop music is known for its intense images of violence and regular references to guns and murder. In 1999, the Center for Substance Abuse Prevention of the U.S. Department of Health and Human Services performed a study of the thousand most popular songs of 1996 and 1997 and discovered that 47 percent of the rap songs in this group contained references to alcohol.

This Code explains the aura of danger, so puzzling to Europeans, surrounding alcohol in American culture. When we drink to excess, on some level we feel as though we are toying with a loaded gun. When we abhor drinking and driving, or frown at drunkenness, it is because we fear what can happen if the gun goes off.

The Code helps explain why teenagers are fascinated with alcohol. At that age, flirting with danger is especially appealing because you feel invulnerable. What better way to prove your invincibility than to play with guns?

Marketing alcohol in America is a dicey business, as liquor companies need to walk a line between being on Code and turning off a large audience (whose cortexes tell them that drinking to excess is socially unacceptable and inherently dangerous), being constructively off Code, and being off Code entirely.

Using gun imagery certainly appeals to youth; Captain Morgan rum seems to be pitching its product in this direction. The pirate on the Captain Morgan bottle wields a sword instead of a gun, but the message is largely the same. Colt .45 malt liquor has found tremendous success within the hip-hop culture, connecting a product with the name of a gun to a community saturated with violent lyrics.

The malt liquor St. Ides took this even further. They created a series of ads using as their spokespeople hip-hop artists, several of whom drew an explicit connection between alcohol and guns. Eric B. and Rakim called St. Ides "bold like a Smith & Wesson." Rappers Erick and Parrish called on their cronies to "hit the bozak [gun] while I take a sip."

Anheuser-Busch promoted Busch beer to outdoorsmen via in-store displays of inflatable Labrador retrievers and banners decorated with scenes of ducks flying above Busch beer cans. They distributed an "Official Busch Hunting Gear" catalog, complete with camouflage beer holders and a floating gun case with the brand's logo.

Earlier, we discussed how advertisers succeed in using fantasy sex to sell their products because of America's fascination with fantasy violence. The proliferation of liquor ads selling sex completes a triangle. The sexual images send unconscious messages of violence, putting the ads on Code for a product that also generates violent messages in our unconscious.

Corona Beer, on the other hand, seems to be making an effort to go constructively off Code in its advertising. Corona ads are filled with soothing images (beaches, palm trees, and so on) with the tagline "Miles away from ordinary." The message here is of transformation, but not a violent one.

Sadly, marketing alcohol by selling quality of crafsmanship seems entirely off Code. It appeals to a small American subculture, in the same way that food magazines appeal to American foodies, but it will never capture the mass market.

A NICE MEAL AND A BOTTLE OF WINE, ANYONE?

The Codes for food and alcohol take us back to one of the recurring themes in our culture: we love things that help us get our jobs done and we fear things that get in the way. All human beings need food to survive. Task-oriented Americans take this literally, regarding food as the fuel to drive their ever-running engines. Alcohol, by contrast, makes you relaxed at best, drunk at worst—neither of which enhances our missions. It is therefore not surprising that we perceive alcohol as something dangerous or even deadly.

As for pleasure, it doesn't make even a fleeting appearance in either of these Codes. It's tough to take time for pleasure when you've got a job to do.

Chapter 9

JUST PUT THAT ALIBI ON
MY GOLD CARD

The Codes for Shopping and Luxury

We have seen in the Codes the power of the reptilian brain at work. Yet even when we allow our reptilian brains to guide us, we still make an effort to appease our cortexes. To do so, we make use of alibis.

Alibis give "rational" reasons for doing the things we do. Think about some of the earlier Codes we've addressed. Our alibi for abstaining from casual sex is that we fear for our reputations or we fear sexually transmitted diseases, but our unconscious tells us that we fear violence. Our alibi for getting fat is that we love food or that our schedules don't allow us to eat in a healthy manner, but our unconscious knows that we're checking out.

Alibis make us feel better about what we do because they feel logical and socially acceptable. Whenever I present a client with a Code, I also present him with an alibi or two gleaned from the discovery sessions. These are important to the client, because an effective marketing campaign needs to consider the alibis while addressing the Code. For instance, a food packager who focused only on the effectiveness of the fuel in its product without also suggesting that the product tasted good would leave an important selling point unstated. Alibis address the "conventional wisdom" about an archetype, the kind of thing you are likely to hear in a focus group. While you can't *believe* what people say, it would be a mistake not to *listen to* it and incorporate it into your message.

At a personal level, an alibi often has credibility even if it is not the reason why a person does what he does. Your schedule really might make it difficult for you to eat as well as you should. It isn't the reason you're fat, but once you address why you are checking out, you still need to come up with an eating plan that accommodates your hours. Just as companies need to consider both the Code and the alibi, so do individuals. Any long-held excuse has at least a modicum of validity. On this point, the alibis for shopping and luxury are highly instructive.

TAKING A TRIP TO THE REST OF THE WORLD

When Procter & Gamble commissioned a discovery on shopping, the alibis quickly emerged. Throughout the sessions, women repeatedly said that they shopped to buy goods for themselves and their families and that they liked going shopping because it gave them the opportunity to discover the best products to purchase. This is very logical and exactly what one might expect to hear. It is practical. Households need food and clothing, laundry detergent and toilet paper. Going to the local shopping center to buy these things is an efficient way to compare products and supply your home with the best you can afford.

Still, this is only an alibi.

In the third hour of the sessions, when the participants relaxed and remembered their first imprint and their most important and most recent memories of shopping, the message behind the alibi began to emerge.

My first memory of shopping was going to the mall with my mother when I was six or seven and seeing my best friend, Lisa,

THE CULTURE CODE   157

there. While our mothers did whatever they were doing, Lisa and I wandered around behind them, looking at all of the stuff we wanted to buy and pretending to try on grown-up clothes. After that, we made our mothers buy us lunch together. I cried when we had to go home.—*a thirty-year-old woman*

Nothing will be more powerful to me than the first time I got to go to the mall with my friends and without my mother. I was twelve at the time and I convinced my mother to let me ride the bus downtown with two of my school friends. We ran into another bunch of girls from school while we were there and spent the entire day looking at everything—including things in stores we could never afford. The mall had this big seating area and we hung out there for a while as well just talking about boys and other people we knew.—*a twenty-seven-year-old woman*

After my first child was born, I had to stay in bed for a while due to complications from the birth. My sister stayed with me during this time and she did all the shopping, cooking, and cleaning. I really appreciated it, but I also really felt shut in. A couple of days after my sister went home, I went to the store for the first time. I was a bit nervous about this, because I hadn't been out in a public place with my son yet and I didn't know what to expect. I had visions of him crying uncontrollably while I tried to pick out something for dinner. When we got into the store, though, he was an absolute angel. People kept coming up to look at him and I felt very proud. We wound up rolling up and down the aisles and I got enough food for the week. It felt so good to be up and around again.—*a thirty-eight-year-old woman*

A couple of weeks ago, my best friend and I drove an hour and a half to go to a new mall that just opened. It was the most amazing place I've ever seen. It had hundreds of stores, a huge food court, a twenty-theater multiplex, and even a Ferris wheel. I thought I'd died and gone to heaven. We couldn't think of where to start. Everything I wanted—and a lot of things I didn't know I wanted—was right there.—*a forty-eight-year-old woman*

A few years ago, my husband's company moved us to "middle-of-nowhere" North Carolina. We had a beautiful house in a town with lovely people, but I had to drive a hundred miles just to find a decent shoe store—which I did on a regular basis. Six months ago, he was transferred back to Philadelphia. Our house isn't as nice as the house was in North Carolina, but the shopping is glorious. I feel like I've returned to the real world. —*a fifty-five-year-old woman*

The content of these stories varied in details (running around with friends, taking a baby out for the first time, driving a hundred miles for good shopping), but the *structure* of the stories bore a consistent theme: "I cried when we had to go home." "We spent the entire day looking at everything—including things in stores we could never afford." "It felt so good to be up and around again." "I thought I'd died and gone to heaven." "I feel like I've returned to the real world." There was a sense in these stories that shopping was a joyous, uplifting enterprise, edifying in ways far beyond purchases made or products handled. Shopping was an emotional, rewarding, and necessary experience.

The American Culture Code for shopping is RECONNECTING WITH LIFE.

This is the real message behind the alibi. Yes, we shop because we need things, but shopping is more than a means of meeting material needs. It is a social experience. It is a way for us to get out of our homes and back into the world. It is something we can do with friends and loved ones. It is a way for us to encounter a wide variety of people and learn what's new in the world—new products, new styles, and new trends—beyond what we see on television. We go shopping, and it seems as though the entire world is there.

This Code taps into the adolescent component of our culture. We all want to "go out and play." We aren't going to learn anything sitting alone at home. Only when we go out into the world do we discover anything new about life.

The Code is present in an image of an early era in our culture that has achieved mythic power. In frontier days, women spent most of their time at the homestead, running the household. Their trips into town to buy groceries and other goods often supplied their only contact with other people—their one chance to reconnect with life.

Interestingly, while buying is the alibi many of us use when we go shopping, there is a significant difference, in the American mind, between shopping and buying. Buying is about carrying out a specific mission—purchasing groceries, picking up a book you saw on television, getting your kid new sneakers. It is a task. Shopping, on the other hand, is a wondrous experience filled with discovery, revelation, and surprise.

When the Internet revolution began, pundits suggested that online shopping would spell the demise of brick-and-mortar stores. E commerce is certainly a burgeoning segment of the marketplace (according to a recent report, dollars spent online increased 31 percent from June 2004 to May 2005), but it was a rare retailer that went out of business because its customers shifted over to the Internet. In fact, many of the most powerful online retailers are those that also have a significant presence in the brick-and-mortar world. Nearly 40 percent of all online sales come from the websites of traditional retailers, more than any other category of store. Consumers like the synergy between the buying they can do online and the shopping they can do at a retail outlet. In a discovery done for a major American retailer, participants corroborated this in both the first and third hours.

This makes perfect sense. The Internet fulfills our need to perform the task of buying, allowing us either to make a purchase online or do the research necessary to comparison-shop and learn more about a product. For instance, people learn a great deal about cars online, including the price the dealer pays, but though they can actually complete the purchase via the Internet, overwhelmingly they choose to go to a dealership instead. Haggling and "beating" the dealer with their research is an integral part of the exercise. While it offers convenience and flexibility, the Internet cannot provide the kind of shopping experience that Americans want. It doesn't allow us to get out into the world and reconnect with life.

While shopping is wondrous and life-affirming, buying sends a very different unconscious message, especially to women. Buying signals the end of shopping, the point at which you sever your connection with the world and go back home. While you are shopping, you have access to myriad choices. When you buy, you narrow your choices down to one. I used to be amazed and frustrated by the sight of my wife shopping for three hours, making dozens of selections, and then deciding after all that time to purchase nothing. With my new glasses, though, I understand this perfectly. She was after the reconnection, not the product, and when she decided not to buy, her alibi for going shopping again in the near future—that she still needed the product—remained.

Retailers need to consider this shopping/buying tension. If women dread the checkout line because it signals the end of the shopping experience, then stores need to revolutionize the buying experience. Retailers need to find a way to enable their customers to avoid this symbolic end of the shopping day, perhaps by registering their credit card information when they enter the store. The consumer can then walk out with whatever she wants and sensors will record the purchase. If the retailer also has a very liberal return policy, the consumer will feel as if the shopping experience never really ends—she can take home the items that interest her without the melancholy of checking out, "live with them" for a few days, and then return whatever she doesn't need. This even offers the consumer an alibi for returning to the store. Nordstrom has based part of its reputation on its willingness to take items back with no questions asked. They've turned shopping into an open-ended experience.

Like so many of our Codes, shopping means something different in other cultures. Procter & Gamble asked me to do the same discovery in France, and I learned that the French Culture Code for shopping is LEARNING YOUR CULTURE. The French consider shopping an educational experience in which older family members pass knowledge down through the generations. A mother will take her daughter shopping, teach her how to buy things, and through this process teach her how the culture operates. She'll explain why it is important to buy bread, wine, and cheese at the same time (because they will be consumed together) or why certain colors and textures go together while others do not. A key phrase in the French shopping experience is "*ça ne se fait pas*," meaning "One isn't supposed to do that." French women learn the rules of life by shopping with their mothers and grandmothers, and they become acculturated as they do. Shopping is the school of the culture.

TAKING THE TIME TO RECONNECT

From a business perspective, one is on Code whenever one underscores shopping as a joyful, life-affirming experience. Making shoppers feel that they can browse without pressure to make a buying decision is a very good thing, as is creating a space for them to linger (many bookstores have done this by adding cafés). Establishing a store as a place where people can gather and reconnect is definitely on Code. If you can include a setting where children (or, often, *husbands* and children) can play, this is even better. Children are focused on "now time," which makes pleasurable shopping difficult. Anything that can distract them in a safe environment will enhance a mother's shopping pleasure.

With the exception of convenience stores, emphasizing the efficiency with which the consumer can make purchases is off Code. While telling people they can get in and out of your store quickly seems to make sense at the cortical level, it flies directly in the face of the Code. Telling shoppers they can have a fast shopping experience in your store is a little bit like trying to sell a thirty-second massage or half a piece of chocolate.

For consumers, your new glasses can be very liberating. Maybe you feel guilty about how long you take to pick something out. Maybe your spouse gives you a hard time about being indecisive. It turns out that your behavior is on Code and his is not. Enjoy the experience. Reconnect with life. Don't buy anything if you don't feel like it. You can always come up with another alibi to get back to the store.

WHAT A $5,000 REFRIGERATOR AND AN OFFICERS' MESS HAVE IN COMMON

We are just as likely to have a practical alibi for purchasing luxury items. We need the fully loaded SUV because winter roads are difficult to navigate. We need the hand-tailored suit because it is important to make a good first impression on clients. We need to buy the oversized diamond for our fiancée because we want her to know how much we love her.

Indeed, most of our favorite luxury items are functional. Americans seek luxury in things they can use: huge homes, top-of-the-line automobiles, professional-quality kitchens, designer clothes, and the like. In a culture with such a strong bias for action, we even design our vacations to restore us so we can get back to work.

Other cultures find luxury in things that are less functional. The Italian culture—a culture imprinted strongly by its veneration of great patrons of the arts—defines luxury via an item's artistic value. Something is luxurious if it is highly refined, elegant, and well designed. Luxury is a product created by an artist. The home of a wealthy person in Italy is filled with gorgeous pieces of art selected by the owner or his ancestors. A luxury item might be a necklace, or even a gorgeously designed handbag. It is not, however, a refrigerator.

As we have discussed elsewhere in this book, the French culture puts a premium on the attainment of pleasure. Luxury in France represents the freedom to do nothing and to own useless things—things that provide beauty and harmony, but have no practical function. A common French expression translates as "What is useless is what I cannot live without." For example, a French woman will buy a very expensive scarf and then wear it draped on her shoulder. The scarf is useless (or, at the very least, redundant) in this position, but it is luxurious. To the French, luxury is something that offers the highest level of pleasure—the finest food, the most elegant clothing, the most refined fragrances. The French culture believes you are living a life of luxury if you can enjoy things that others (peasants, the working class, Americans) cannot enjoy.

The British use luxury to underscore their sense of detachment. They'll join exclusive clubs where they can show one another how unimpressed they are with their own status. They'll play polo matches, lose, and then tell everyone how sanguine they are about losing because winning wasn't the point. Their aristocrats are notoriously unattractive and unadorned, their castles unheated, their chairs uncushioned.

When Richemont and Boeing wanted to crack the Code for luxury, Americans revealed that luxury could be had a number of ways:

One of the first things I had to do after getting my first corporate job was to buy a car. I was new in town and had no way to
get around. I was living on a tight budget back then and definitely couldn't afford anything fancy, but I test drove a couple of
high-end automobiles anyway. I settled on a Honda back then,
but a year ago, I got the promotion that put me over the top.
One of the first things I did was buy the Jaguar I always wanted.
The feeling in that car is just incredible and I know I deserve it.
—*a forty-one-year-old man*

My most powerful memory of luxury is the trip my husband and
I took to Tuscany five years ago. We'd both been working incredibly long hours at our offices and the last few vacations were
quickly thrown together and unsatisfying. This time, we set up
our schedules right and then we looked at our bank balances
and decided we could handle it. We stayed in amazing places—
even a castle for three nights—and did everything top-of-the-
line. It was the first time in years that I felt like I was getting
something back for all of my hard work.—*a thirty-six-year-old
woman*

My wife does most of the cooking in our home, but I'm a primo
grill chef and I take over during the summer. When our old grill
gave out two years ago, I decided I wanted to go all-out. Hey,
what's the point in making the money if you can't do something
with it? I got this huge stainless-steel beauty and then decided I
wanted to redo the whole patio setup to go around it. It cost us
a ton, but when I'm making steaks, the whole neighborhood
lines up for a taste.—*a fifty-four-year-old man*

When I was in Aruba recently, I bought myself a beautiful thick
gold bracelet. The prices were so good there that I decided to

splurge. It's the kind of thing my husband should buy for me, except I'm not married. I figured it was time to stop waiting and to get myself a big bauble.—*a forty-two-year-old woman*

My first memory of luxury was being the first kid I knew to get a PlayStation. My parents bought it for me for getting straight As. Of course, a year later, everyone in the world seemed to have one, but for a while all of my friends had to come to my house if they wanted to play and that made me feel pretty special. I felt especially good knowing that I had earned it.—*a twenty-two-year-old man*

The third-hour stories were all over the place in terms of subject matter. Where one participant considered a car to represent luxury, another saw luxury as manifested in elegant jewelry and a third in a piece of hot new electronic equipment. The key phrases, though, were very consistent and created a pattern. "Just incredible and I know I deserve it." "Getting something back for all my hard work." "What's the point in making the money if you can't do something with it?" Whatever you're buying, the point seems to be that you deserve it.

There is no noble class in America. We don't have titles to indicate our station in society. This is not and has never been the American way. At the same time, though, we have an incredibly strong work ethic, an intense passion to succeed, and, because we are an adolescent culture, a powerful desire to let people know what we've done. Since no one is going to knight us when we make our mark, we need something else to indicate our rank in the world. In addition, since we believe that you are never finished growing, our rank should come in stages, reaching a higher level the more we accomplish.

The way we show our rank in American society is through our luxury items, and the American Culture Code for luxury is MILITARY STRIPES.

In many ways, this Code is an extension of the Code for money. Military stripes are a form of proof, something you wear on your sleeve for all to respect. These Codes are very closely linked, not only because one needs money to buy luxury items but because when Americans attain the "proof" of money, they use luxury items to show it off.

With military stripes, though, there is the added notion of levels—the more stripes one has, the higher one's rank. Indeed, there are levels of luxury, just as there are levels in the military. A Lexus is a luxury car, but so is a Maserati and so is a Bentley. Donna Karan designs luxury clothing, but Dolce & Gabbana and Escada are even more exclusive. Beachfront property in Florida states that you've arrived at a certain level. A mansion in Greenwich, Connecticut, suggests another and a penthouse on Fifth Avenue in Manhattan yet another. These levels indicate the "stripes" you've earned with your accomplishments.

What is the purpose of these stripes? Largely, it is recognition; not recognition of how much money you have, though, but of your goodness. At the unconscious level, Americans believe that good people succeed, that success is bestowed upon you by God. Your success demonstrates that God loves you.

When you attain this level of approval from your Maker, you want to be treated accordingly. Service is an important component of luxury. Again, there is a connection with the military. A military officer has certain privileges that lower-ranking soldiers don't have. He has access to the officers' mess; people salute him when he passes. Similarly, as we achieve higher rank in the civilian world, we expect privileges and services unavailable to the average American. We want a personal shopper at Saks. We want a black American Express card. We want a tuxedoed staff to wait on us at the best tables in the best restaurants. We want to skip the long lines at airports. In America, service is a luxury item and we are willing to pay exorbitant prices for it. We'll spend $400 for a meal at Alain Ducasse because the restaurant treats us in a deluxe fashion. We'll spend $4,000 for a first-class ticket from New York to Los Angeles because of the quality of the service while we are in the air.

Like the military, luxury comes not only in different ranks, but also in different "branches," and the branch we choose says a good deal about how we want the world to perceive us. A Volvo, a safari vacation, and a large donation to the NEA send a message very different from that sent by a Suburban, a week at a stock-car-racing fantasy camp, and a big check to the NRA.

To succeed in marketing luxury items in America, a company needs to make it clear that it is selling "stripes." Branding is extremely important. A luxury item has value only if others know how luxurious it is. Rolex has done a brilliant job of establishing its products as the signature luxury watches in America, with distinctive design and ceaseless marketing efforts announcing how valuable a Rolex watch is. Similarly, Ralph Lauren has done masterful work branding Polo. The logo of a polo player connects with everything from medieval class status (when nobility rode and everyone else walked) to the American cowboy mythos, and consumers can wear it like a blazon, announcing their ability to afford such a luxury item in a way that most Americans can understand.

Equally important in marketing luxury in America is the notion of progression. Because Americans equate health with movement, there is a strong belief in this culture that you are never finished growing, that as long as you are active, you are always in transition to your next big accomplishment. When we achieve a certain level of success, we rarely say "I've arrived; I'm done." Most of us immediately think about achieving greater success. We regard our luxury items similarly. Now that we can afford the Lexus, we want to be in a position to afford the Bentley. A company that offers multiple levels of luxury has the opportunity to keep its customers as they ascend. Tiffany does this superbly. The "little blue box" is practically synonymous with luxury in America, but Tiffany offers its luxury at a variety of price points. You can get the distinctively designed silver earrings for a little more than $200; you can get the gold-and-diamond bracelet for a little more than $6,000; you can get the diamond-and-emerald ring for $2 million, or you can choose from a wide variety of levels in between. By offering customers the opportunity to experience Tiffany luxury at a relatively affordable level while showing them the loftier levels at the same time, the company builds a lifelong bond.

Of paramount importance to selling luxury in America is supplementing your product with luxury service. Treating your high-end customers as though they are members of an "officers' club" is precisely on Code. Once an American has earned his stripes, he wants to be treated accordingly. He wants to be seen as someone who is actively involved in achieving significant things and he wants to know that you realize his time and presence are valuable. The Ritz-Carlton hotel chain was one of the first to do an excellent job with this, offering its Club Level guests a dedicated concierge staff, exclusive meal service, and a private lounge.

In addition, one must always remember that we need our alibis. Our cultural unconscious will lead us to respond positively to luxury items that offer us "stripes," but our cortexes must be satisfied as well. We'll buy a $4,000 professional cooktop, but only if you convince us that it will make our kitchen more functional. We'll spend an extra $200 a day for spa services in our four-star hotel, but only if you convince us that we'll emerge refreshed and ready to resume our mission.

Certain industries have skillfully connected alibis to luxury items. Corporate jets are an utterly luxurious way to travel, but the leasing companies understand that we need an alibi. Therefore, they underscore how much time busy executives save by using a corporate jet, how those executives can use that time to work, and how the environment the leasing company creates on the jets allows executives to keep working.

Earlier, we saw that the diamond industry sells romance on one hand and "investment value" on the other. The latter serves as an attempt to provide an alibi. The notion here is that you'll be more willing to buy that $10,000 engagement ring if you can tell yourself it will appreciate over time.

AS LONG AS I HAVE AN ALIBI, I'M COVERED

Alibis help us to make sense of the messages the Codes send us. Few of us are aware enough of our motivations to understand that our excitement over that pending shopping trip comes from the reconnection that trip will provide. What we tell ourselves instead is that we *need* things—shoes for an upcoming social event, clothes for the kids' new school year, a new range before the old one stops working, a new car because the other one is coming off lease. Similarly, few of us acknowledge that we're buying "stripes" when we buy our luxury items. Instead, the car is for entertaining clients; the built-in swimming pool is for the children and their friends.

Alibis work because they seem legitimate. They give us good reason to do things we want to do anyway. We can reconnect with life. We can exhibit our stripes. And our cortexes won't give us the least bit of trouble.

Chapter 10

WHO DO THESE UPSTARTS THINK THEY ARE?

The Codes for America in Other Cultures

J ust as different cultures view various archetypes differently, they also view America according to their own Culture Codes. Understanding the Code for America in different cultures has a huge impact on how a product, a concept, or indeed a foreign policy will be received there. With marketing in mind, a collection of American corporations, including DuPont, Boeing, and Procter & Gamble sought to discover the Code for America in France, Germany, and England.

America has always had its detractors. However, the number and threat level of these detractors seems to have ratcheted up in the early years of the twenty-first century. In a poll by the Pew Research Center released in late June 2005, unfavorable opinions of America ranged from 29 percent in India to 79 percent in Jordan. The majority of those polled in most of our ally countries had an unfavorable opinion of America, including 57 percent in France, 59 percent in Germany, and 59 percent in Spain. The results in strongly Muslim countries, like those in Jordan, were unsurprising, with 77 percent in Turkey and Pakistan and 58 percent in Lebanon having an unfavorable opinion. Ratings were especially low for America when participants were asked about American foreign policy and George W.

Bush's reelection. When asked whether U.S. foreign policy takes into account the interests of others, only 38 percent said yes in Germany and 32 percent in Great Britain, while Poland (13 percent), France (18 percent), Spain (19 percent), and Russia (21 percent) were even more negative. Meanwhile, the majority of those polled in Spain (60 percent), Great Britain (62 percent), France (74 percent), and Germany (77 percent) said they had a less favorable opinion of America after the reelection of George W. Bush.

America's problems with France in recent years have been well documented. As it happens, the strong sense of anti-Americanism in France (and, specifically, the hatred of George W. Bush) directly relates to the conflicts in the Culture Codes of the two countries. George W. Bush is the quintessential American leader. He's brash, with a strong adolescent streak, he's uncultured, he's an action figure who shoots first and asks questions later, and he's not concerned with getting things right the first time. The French are thinkers; they believe that intellect and reason provide the answers to big questions. In other words, George W. Bush is the antithesis of everything that guides the French on an unconscious level. It is no mystery that French-American relations are at a historic low. Here is what the French had to say in our discovery:

> I keep thinking that Americans are going to fail terribly sometime soon. How can you succeed when you know so little about how the world works? Somehow, though, they tend to wind up on top. It's a complete mystery to me.—*a forty-year-old French man*

> The first thing I think of when I think of Americans is the moon landing. That really was a remarkable thing to see. To think that they conquered the bounds of this planet and landed on another is just incredible to me. When I think about that and then I think

about how many stupid things they do now, I have trouble making sense of it.—*a sixty-four-year-old French man*

I spent a summer in California when I was in college. I went to Disneyland, and Universal Hollywood, and I went to movie studios and took a tour of the stars' houses. It is so unreal there, but I have to admit it was quite fun. That is America to me. —*a twenty-three-year-old French woman*

When I think of America, I think of *Star Wars,* Superman, comic books, and *Star Trek.* The food is terrible, but you have to give them credit for having great imaginations.—*a twenty-seven-year-old French man*

Participants in France talked about the confusion that stemmed from their belief that they were supposed to illuminate the world with their ideas but that the Americans were actually doing it. They truly didn't understand how this was possible. Consistently, participants told of their conviction that we were unfit to lead the world, but then grudgingly acknowledged our ability to learn from mistakes and come back stronger. When asked for their first imprint of America, many mentioned our landing on the moon, while others spoke of Hollywood, fantasy, toys, and imagination. They characterized us as childlike and naïve, but powerful at the same time. When the French spoke of Americans, it was almost as though they were speaking about an alien race.

The Code for America in France is SPACE TRAVELERS.

Knowledge of the Code helps put several things into perspective. That the French see us as intergalactic voyagers explains why they feel they can't relate to us, why they think our motivations are different from theirs. In addition, it helps explain why they see us as usurpers. In their minds, we've landed on their world and are trying to impose our culture and our values on them; and because we are "travelers," we don't have the same commitment to the well-being of the planet that they have. How could we really know what is important for humanity when we are not fully human?

In Germany, participants spoke of Americans with a certain sense of fascination:

> They do things in such a haphazard fashion. It is almost as though they are forever improvising, just doing the first things that come into their minds. In spite of this, though, I don't know, it works. They get things done. They have an incredible ability to do the right thing.—*a thirty-six-year-old German man*

> I saw a lot of American soldiers when I was growing up. People with guns scare me, especially if they aren't from my country. Still, they seemed very nice to us, especially the children. They would joke with children and teach them how to act like "good soldiers." I always found that touching.—*a fifty-seven-year-old German woman*

> Americans are cowboys. All of them are cowboys. They might wear business suits, but they still act like cowboys. They aren't as smart or disciplined as we are, but they have an impressive ability to do what they set out to do.—*a fifty-year-old German man*

> I hate to admit it, but I'm not sure where we'd be without America. They saved us from ourselves in our darkest hour.—*a forty-two-year-old German woman*

Like the French, the Germans see us as not being one of them, but they focus more on our accomplishments. They acknowledge that we are powerful leaders and the foremost world authority, but they do so with a sense of disbelief. Germans see themselves as superior in education, engineering, and creating order. They see Americans as primitive, yet they understand that America has been able to do things on a world level that they have not—and this confounds them. One subject that came up repeatedly in the discovery sessions was our friendliness to children. America's attitude toward its children and the children of the world strikes a resonant chord with Germans. They've imprinted us as liberators and benevolent cowboys.

The Code for America in Germany is JOHN WAYNE.

The Code helps explain why American-German relations were so good for so long (in 2000, 78 percent of Germans polled had a favorable opinion of the United States) and why it is strained now. The image of John Wayne is of the strong, friendly stranger who helps save a town from trouble and then moves on with no expectation of thanks or remuneration. John Wayne is a tough guy. He's "the law." He never, however, shoots first. In this context, our actions in Iraq are off Code to Germans because they believe that we "shot first" there, embarking on a military response before exhausting all diplomatic solutions.

The English have their own way of seeing us:

> I have several American friends. I find them endlessly entertaining. When I go to America, I know I'm going to eat too much, drink too much, stay up too late, and speak twice as loudly as I normally speak. I couldn't live that way all the time, but it is A LOT of fun.—*a thirty-two-year-old English man*

> Everything about America is big. The country is big, the people are big, their ambitions are *very* big, and their appetite for everything is big. I've never been there, but I imagine everyone living in a huge house and driving gigantic cars.—*an eighteen-year-old English woman*

It's easy to think of Americans as somewhat beneath us. Their accents are ridiculous (and they insist on using their voices at such high volume), they all seem like a bunch of bounding children, they consider "history" to be anything that took place in the past decade, and they all weigh too much. If they are beneath us, though, why have they accomplished so much? They seem to understand something we fail to understand.—*a fifty-five-year-old English man*

I always know when an American is in my shop. They don't even have to open their mouths for me to know. It's in their eyes. Americans want everything.—*a forty-eight-year-old English woman*

English participants spoke of us as big, loud, powerful, vulgar, extreme, and determined to win at any cost. They talked about our lack of restraint, our lack of tradition, and our lack of a class system, while at the same time admiring our confidence, passion, record of success, and can-do attitude. When asked to recall their first imprint of America, participants consistently spoke of vastness—the size of the country, the size of its symbols (the Statue of Liberty, Mount Rushmore, the Empire State Building), and the size of its influence on the world. In speaking about America, the notion of quantity came up with great regularity.

The English Code for America is UNASHAMEDLY ABUNDANT.

This helps explain why the majority of English polled (55 percent) have a favorable opinion of America (though the proportion is down precipitously from the 83 percent rating in 2000). The English expect us to seek abundance in everything. They expect us to be extreme and to try to win at any cost. Therefore, our present foreign policy is on Code for them.

MAKING A PROFITABLE MARRIAGE

Now that the companies involved in this study had the French, German, and English Codes for America, it was essential that they not run away from their "American-ness" in building a marketing strategy in each culture. If the English expect abundance from Americans, it is important to highlight that. Products should come "fully loaded" and "super-sized." If the Germans expect John Wayne, products should help "save the day" without asking anyone to change who they are (remember the successful marketing campaign for the Jeep Wrangler, which capitalized on that car's Code as "liberator"). If the French expect us to be space travelers, then the products we bring them should have an otherworldly quality: they should feel new and unusual.

But knowing the foreign Codes for America still does not ensure success in that market. Any marketing strategy in a foreign culture must also be cognizant of what a culture thinks of itself.

The French Code for France is IDEA. Raised on stories of great French philosophers and thinkers, French children imprint the value of ideas as paramount and refinement of the mind as the highest goal.

The English Code for England is CLASS. There is a strong sense among the English that they are of a higher social stratum than other people. This arises from England's long history of world leadership ("the sun never sets on the British Empire") and from the messages passed down from generation to generation that being English is a special privilege that one receives at birth.

The German Code for Germany is perhaps best illustrated in a story.

Lego, the Danish toy company, found instant success with their interlocking blocks in the German market, while sales foundered in the United States. Why?

The company's management believed that one of the primary reasons for their success was the quality of the instructions they provided inside each box that helped children build the specific item (a car, a spaceship) that a particular box of blocks was meant to build. The instructions were quite a breakthrough in the field: precise, colorful, and refreshingly clear. They made construction with Lego blocks not only simple, but in some ways magical. If one followed the path through the instructions, tiny plastic pieces methodically turned into something grander.

American children could not have cared less. They would tear into the boxes, glance fleetingly at the instructions (if they looked at them at all), and immediately set out on a construction project of their own. They seemed to be having a wonderful time, but they were as likely to build, say, a fort, as they were to build the automobile for which the blocks were intended. And when they were done, they would tear their fort apart and start over from scratch. To Lego's dismay, a single box of Legos could last for years.

In Germany, however, Lego's strategy worked exactly as intended. German children opened a box of Legos, sought out the instructions, read them carefully, and then sorted the pieces by color. They began building, comparing their assembly progress to the crisp, helpful illustrations in the instruction booklet. When they were finished, they had an exact duplicate of the product shown on the cover of the box. They showed it to Mother, who clapped approvingly and put the model on a shelf. *Now the children needed another box.*

Without knowing it, Lego had tapped into the Culture Code for Germany itself: ORDER. Over many generations, Germans perfected bureaucracy in an effort to stave off the chaos that came to them in wave after wave, and Germans are imprinted early on with this most powerful of codes. That imprint makes children reach dutifully for the instructions, and that Code prevents them from immediately destroying their neat construction in order to build it anew. Lego's elegant, full-color instructions had tapped into the German Code in a way that assured repeat sales.

Given both Codes—the Code for the home culture and the Code for the foreign culture—a company should be well armed to succeed.

Several years ago, AT&T attempted to get the contract for France's national phone service. Their primary competition was the Swedish company Ericsson. AT&T's pitch focused on how big and powerful it was and how it could come in and save the flagging French telephone system. They failed to acknowledge either the French Code for America (by presenting something new or unusual) or the French Code for France (by acknowledging that they could work with the ideas the French already had in place). When the Ericsson people made their pitch, they appealed first to the French Code. They thanked the French for giving them their monarchy (in a Napoleonic brainstorm of turning the country over to the young general Jean Bernadotte, who became King Charles XIV and led Sweden into the modern era). By starting this way, Erickson acknowledged its understanding of the French culture and showed that the company respected it and could work well within it. They received the contract.

Chrysler (which is still perceived as an American company because all research and development for Chrysler products comes out of Detroit) did a much better job of navigating the Codes when it introduced the PT Cruiser to France. They fulfilled the American role as space travelers by introducing a car that looked like nothing else on French roads. They then marketed the car in a way that was completely on Code for the French. Their ads spoke of the 150 new ideas that went into the creation of the PT Cruiser, with different ads detailing several of these ideas. The French, of course, responded to this. Even though the PT Cruiser costs much more in France than it does in America, it is hugely popular there.

The bottom line for business is that it is not possible for an American company to succeed in the world marketplace with one global message. How could one strategy possibly address IDEA/SPACE TRAVELERS, ORDER/JOHN WAYNE, and CLASS/UNASHAMEDLY ABUN-DANT at the same time? A global strategy requires customizing for each culture, though it is always important that the strategy embrace "American-ness."

When Jeep relaunched the Wrangler in France and Germany using the "liberator" pitch, sales increased significantly. The pitch worked because it was on Code in terms of how those countries saw themselves and us. In France, the ads played up the Wrangler's unique styling to appeal to the national fascination with ideas. In addition, the Wrangler's off-road capabilities subtly suggest the notion of space travel, of breaking through the bonds of our atmosphere. In Germany, focusing the marketing campaign on the Jeep's place in history was an on-Code reminder of the order restored to that country after World War II, and of the John Wayne–like part the Jeep played in liberating Germany from the Third Reich.

In England, the marketing campaign needed to be very different. The English didn't have the experience of American soldiers liberating them. In addition, their own Land Rover dominated SUV sales in this category in England. Understanding the country Codes, the company chose not to push hard with the Wrangler in England, but to position the upscale Grand Cherokee as the Jeep of choice instead. The campaign showed a couple taking a fully loaded Grand Cherokee from their London house to their country estate. The presentation of the car's numerous high-end features was an illustration of unashamed abundance, while the beautiful house in London and the sprawling country estate emphasized class. The ad was right on Code, and it helped Jeep gain ground on the Land Rover.

LIVING ON CODE

America and Americans send different messages to different cultures around the world. People within those cultures sometimes see in these messages something they long for, something that is missing from their lives. When a person sees something in a foreign culture that feels more consistent with his or her own worldview, moving to that culture can make a great deal of sense.

I was born in France, but like everyone else in the world, I had no choice of homeland. From the time I was very young, I knew that parts of the French culture failed to fit me properly. The French are extremely critical, they are pessimistic, they are jealous of what others have, and they put little value on personal success. When I told people there that I wanted to build a large business based on new ideas, they sneered and called me a megalomaniac.

The American culture seemed to offer so many of the things I wanted from life, especially in building a career. When I decided to emigrate, François Mitterrand was president of France and he'd frozen the assets of any French citizen leaving the country. Therefore, when I arrived in New York, I had no money. I also had no place to live and my English was very poor. I'd come to America to do work on archetypes, and few people had any idea what I was even talking about.

I knew a few French immigrants in New York and I went to see them as soon as I arrived. They welcomed me, offering me a place to stay, some money, and the use of a car. When I told them about what I planned to do for a living, they encouraged me and told me they were sure I would succeed. As happy as I was to hear these words, the first thought that came to mind was "Are you sure you're French?" These people, who'd been living in America for a few years, were utterly different from the French I knew in France. They were optimistic, helpful, generous, and enthusiastic about new opportunities.

In other words, they were American. Yes, they'd embraced the American culture, but in addition, like me, they had many of these traits already and came here because they knew they would be surrounded by like-minded people. The French who were lazy and lacked imagination stayed in Europe. The ones with guts and determination came here. These people found "home" by moving elsewhere. Their homeland was an accident of birth; they found a permanent place to live when they left it to come to America.

While America does an exemplary job of embracing and assimilating immigrants, Americans can also find their "true home" culture elsewhere. The actress Gwyneth Paltrow, who now lives in England with her British rock-star husband, was recently quoted as saying "I've always been drawn to Europe. America is such a young country, with an adolescent swagger about it." Clearly, the American culture doesn't resonate with Paltrow as the English one does.

As with corporations, the key to successful immigration (here or elsewhere) is connecting with the Code of the local culture. An intellectual from any culture would find France stimulating. A control freak would resonate strongly with the German culture.

For a company breaking into a foreign market or an individual looking for the ideal place to live, the most important thing is to connect with the Code.

Chapter 11

PARTING OF THE RED SEA OPTIONAL

The Code for the American Presidency

I n 1789, when the Electoral College chose George Washington to run the fledgling United States of America, the electors asked him how he would like to be addressed. They suggested traditional terms—"Your Excellency," "Your Majesty," "Sire." Washington responded by saying that he wanted to be called "Mr. President," and thus he set in motion a distinctly American approach to governmental leadership. The new president had no interest in becoming king. He'd recently led his people in an epic battle—against terrible odds— to free themselves from a king, and he and the other Founding Fathers realized that the notion of simply replacing the old boss with a new version of the same thing was inconsistent with the tenets of this emerging country. George Washington became "Mr. President," and in so doing made a tremendously powerful imprint on the American culture.

The American presidency placed the finishing touch on the rebellion against British rule. Unlike earlier historical rebels, we did not assassinate the king in order to effect change—instead, we repudiated him and most of what the monarchy represented and fought to break away. In choosing George Washington as president, the electors selected the leader of that rebellion. He wasn't the king; he was the rebel-in-chief. This meshed effectively with a culture in its infancy (young children are all about testing limits and learning for themselves how the world works), and it connects especially well with our current adolescent culture. Like all adolescents, we have little patience for father figures. However, we are happy to follow a rebel as he leads the charge. Several of the twentieth century's most successful presidents had strong rebellious streaks. Bill Clinton was a Washington outsider with decided adolescent tendencies. Ronald Reagan challenged us to re-create America's greatness by leading a "rebellion" to restore tradition. Franklin Roosevelt rebelled against the Depression with the adolescent cry "We have nothing to fear but fear itself."

This is a very powerful notion and one that never existed in history before the founding of America. Our leader is the person who leads the rebellion. This is essential in a culture where health means movement. We are always changing, always moving forward, always reinventing, and we want a president who can direct this process. The president needs to understand what is broken, have a strong idea about how to fix it, and then "rebel" against the problem. The nature of the rebellion is always changing, and we tend to choose the president who understands this best. In the 2000 and 2004 elections, George W. Bush led the rebellion toward the conservative right. Perhaps the next president will rebel by leading the charge back toward the center.

One cannot be a terribly effective rebel if one cannot state clearly (in words or deeds) what one stands for. We expect our presidents to show us that they know where the country needs to go and how to take us there. The first George Bush famously derided "the vision thing," and that cost him dearly in the 1992 election. George Washington understood "the vision thing." So did Thomas Jefferson, Abraham Lincoln, and all the other presidents who resonate in our minds as the greatest to lead our nation.

This is not to say that we always elect a president who has great vision. Sometimes a president doesn't win an election as much as his opponent loses it. In 1976, Jimmy Carter—someone who hardly comes off as a rebel and one who has been more of a visionary in his postpresidency life—defeated Gerald Ford in large part because Americans had such strong negative feelings about the Republican Party after Watergate. In 2000, George W. Bush's "vision thing" was only slightly stronger than his father's had been, but he won the electoral vote (if not the popular vote) because Al Gore failed to inspire the country.

When the George H. W. Bush campaign hired me to discover the Code for the American presidency, I first studied each of our presidents and their opponents to glean how Americans perceived them during the elections. As with everything else, the reptilian always wins. We don't want our presidents to think too much. We want them to respond from the gut, to have a very strong survival instinct. The candidate doesn't need to be extremely reptilian, only more reptilian than his opponent is. In the 2000 election, Bush wasn't a particularly strong reptilian, but his opponent was *very* cortex. In the 2004 election, the differences were even more pronounced; John Kerry was a veritable Mr. Cortex. In the 1996 election, Bill Clinton was both more reptilian *and* more cortex than Bob Dole, as was the case in 1992 when he defeated George Bush. George Bush, however, was more reptilian than the cortex-driven Michael Dukakis. Ronald Reagan was much more reptilian than either Jimmy Carter or Walter Mondale. If one continues to go back through the other presidential elections, you'll note that this pattern is broken only under extreme circumstances, as after Watergate.

In the discovery sessions for the presidency, party affiliation was unimportant. What we sought was how Americans imprinted the archetype of the president.

When I was a little kid, I remember watching a speech by John F. Kennedy with my mother. She told me he was the president of the United States, but I didn't really know what that meant. At the time, I thought the entire world was contained within the United States. What I noticed about JFK was that when he spoke you wanted to pay attention. Back then, I didn't like to watch the news or anything other than cartoons, but I watched President Kennedy. I don't remember what he talked about that day, but I remember feeling really good afterward.—*a thirty-year-old man*

My fifth-grade teacher had this huge picture of President Reagan hanging in the room. When we said the pledge, we were supposed to look at the flag, but I looked at him instead. He just seemed so calm and so powerful. I knew he was taking care of our country.—*an eighteen-year-old woman*

My first memory of the presidency was listening to FDR's voice on the radio. Things were pretty bad for my family (the whole country, really) back then, but I always felt better after I heard FDR speak. There was something about the things he told us that made me feel like everything was going to turn out okay. —*a sixty-two-year-old man*

My most powerful memory of the presidency was working on the first Reagan campaign here in New Jersey. One day, the future president delivered a speech before the New Jersey primary and I was awestruck at his vision and his sense of purpose. He knew what was wrong and he knew how to fix it. After the speech, I got the chance to shake his hand, and I got this incredible feeling of power just being in his presence.—*a forty-year-old woman*

When I was in elementary school, I had to do a report on a president. Up to that point, I didn't care very much about anything

to do with government. I'm not sure I could have told you who the current president was. Since I had to do something, I picked up a book about Abraham Lincoln and it literally changed my life. When I read about what this man did for his country and how he stuck to his convictions because he knew America needed it, I was awestruck. Since I was a teenager, I've been involved in public service at the local level in various ways and I know this is because of what I learned about President Lincoln.
—*a fifty-one-year-old man*

Phrases like "When he spoke you wanted to pay attention," "I knew he was taking care of our country," "He knew what was wrong and he knew how to fix it," and "I was awestruck" created a picture of what we want in our presidents. We want someone with a highly developed vision who makes us pay attention when he speaks. We want someone with a strong reptilian side who can take care of our country. We want someone who can help us rebel against our problems and lead us into the Promised Land because he knows what is wrong and how to fix it.

We don't want a father figure. We want a biblical figure.

The Culture Code for the American presidency is MOSES.

This might come as a surprise to those who don't follow any organized religion, but if you strip away the religious components of the story of Moses, you'll see that he represents the Code for the American presidency aptly: a rebellious leader of his people with a strong vision and the will to get them out of trouble.

Moses also made his people believe they could do the impossible. This is a skill great presidents have possessed, beginning with George Washington himself. Here was a man who led a ragtag, ill-prepared army to victory over the vastly superior British military. Abraham Lincoln convinced America that it could overcome slavery and civil war. Franklin Roosevelt made Americans believe they could conquer the

Depression. Ronald Reagan imbued us with a vision of greatness when we had fallen into despair. These men did this with more than rhetoric or idealism (in fact, idealism is a critical flaw in a president, as we learned with Jimmy Carter). They inspired us to act by convincing us to share their transcendental vision. They gave us directions out of the desert and into the Promised Land.

But we don't expect our presidents to be ideal humans touched by a divine hand, like the biblical Moses. We don't want our presidents to be perfect—most important, we don't want them to consider themselves perfect. As we've already seen, Americans have strong apprehensions about perfection. We are culturally adolescent, and we expect our president to be adolescent as well. We expect him to be connected to the American soul, and that means rarely doing things right the first time. Instead, we expect him to make mistakes, learn from those mistakes, and be better for it. Clinton's presidency was riddled with mistakes (from the botched national health plan to Whitewater to the Monica Lewinsky scandal), but, according to an ABC News/*Washington Post* poll, his approval ratings at the end of his second term were higher than those of any post–World War II president, including Ronald Reagan. When a president can maintain high approval ratings after an impeachment hearing, it is obvious that we aren't looking for perfection.

The Code for the American president is very consistent with the Code for America itself (which we will explore in the next chapter). This makes perfect sense, as a culture could not function effectively if its model for a leader conflicted with its most fundamental Code.

Canadians, for instance, seek leaders who are capable of maintaining the culture. As mentioned earlier, the Canadian Code for Canada is TO KEEP. This Code evolved from the severe Canadian winters. Canadians learned from the beginning to use what they call "winter energy," to act so as to conserve as much energy as possible. They do not seek leaders with vision, capable of making major breakthroughs. Instead, they elect prime ministers who serve as guardians, who voters believe provide the best chance of keeping the Canadian culture the way it is.

The French, on the other hand, rally behind leaders who challenge the system with new ideas (remember, the French Code for France is IDEA). Napoleon and de Gaulle are considered models of French leadership because they faced down the existing system and changed it to better serve the people (though, as we saw with Napoleon, the notion of "serving the people" changed with time).

ON-CODE VOTING

Why do we vote as we do? In many ways, ideology and platform are not the basis of decision. The differences between conservatism and liberalism (to identify the American extremes) in this country are relatively small. While politicians and pundits paint dramatic pictures of an America starkly divided between red and blue states, you've seen throughout this book that there is strong consistency to how we think as a culture. Discovery sessions in Middle America net the same structure as those held in New York, Chicago, and Los Angeles.

Our "differences" are further diminished by America's three-branch system of government. We debate major issues like abortion, gay rights, nuclear power, Social Security, and immigration control for a very long time before we make any movement at all. In fact, it is likely that the debate on any of these issues will extend beyond the term of whichever president we happen to be electing at the time. In addition, if we do move at all, the debate continues, allowing the opportunity for revision or further change. At the same time, many of our most powerful laws exist at the state level, so that Connecticut can authorize same-sex civil unions even as the debate rages at a national level. The beauty of the American Constitution is that our most powerful leaders don't have too much power.

The basic components of the country really do not change very much during one presidential administration. What *does* change is the spirit of the country, the sense of optimism or the lack thereof. This largely relates to the president's ability to fill the shoes of Moses, to make us believe that he can take us to the Promised Land. Neither 2004 presidential candidate was powerfully on Code. George W. Bush was certainly more reptilian than John Kerry, but his inability to inhabit the role of Moses has led to a sense of pessimism in the country and approval ratings that are near historic lows.

There is a sense in which the president is the "entertainer-in-chief." His primary job is to inspire us, to keep our spirits up and to keep us moving in a productive fashion. Presidents who resonate deep down with the American archetype are excellent entertainers-in-chief. This is why actors (Ronald Reagan, Arnold Schwarzenegger, Clint Eastwood, and Jesse Ventura, to name a few) find popularity among the electorate. An on-Code president transcends ideology and moves the country forward in a way that an off-Code president cannot. Many disagreed with the platforms of FDR and Reagan, but both men effected tremendous turnarounds in America's fortunes (particularly its economic fortunes) during their terms. Rebellious visionaries do that.

For the candidates themselves, the Code offers a vivid image of what Americans expect from their chief executives. The "vision thing" is critical, as is the ability to get one's message across and inspire. Americans don't want father figures who tell them what to do, but they do want men (and someday, maybe even soon, women) with a plan they can understand and follow. In addition, they decidedly do not want a president who thinks too much. Except under extraordinary circumstances, the more reptilian candidate always wins. This is something that John Kerry, Michael Dukakis, and many others didn't understand.

Cultures change very slowly, which means Americans will be looking for "Moses" in their president a long time into the future. If we all understand this Code, the election process could be very different in 2008 and beyond.

Chapter 12

NEVER GROWING UP, NEVER GIVING UP

The Code for America

O ver the course of this book, we have explored some of the most fundamental archetypes in American culture and addressed the unconscious Codes at the heart of those archetypes. Some of these unconscious messages have been instructive (as in the Codes for beauty and shopping), some have been cautionary (as in the Codes for love and fat), and some have even been a little scary (as in the Code for sex). All give us a distinctive glimpse of why we do the things we do, and they provide us with a new set of glasses that allows us to view our behavior afresh. In addition, the contrast with Codes of other cultures has taught us that people around the world really are different.

The Code for America encompasses all the other Codes in this book. It addresses the way we think of ourselves from the widest perspective within our culture and touches on the other Codes at least indirectly. Understanding the Code for America helps explain why we think of love as false expectations, health as movement, luxury as military stripes, and the president as Moses.

So how do Americans see America?

Certainly, we see ourselves as "new." As adolescents, we would, of course. There are no ancient parts of America except our forests and canyons. We're always building and renewing, preferring to tear things down rather than preserve. Our place-names even reflect this. You can step into your car in New York and drive into New England, where you'll pass New Haven, New London, and Newton on your way into New Hampshire. Alternatively, you could drive south and see New Hope, Newberry, and Newington on your way to New Orleans.

We also see ourselves as occupants of vast amounts of space. Were you to step into your car again and drive due west, you could drive for a week and still be in America. In Europe, you could drive through four different countries in half a day. This sense of size pervades our culture. Just as the Japanese are the masters of micro-culture because they must fit a huge number of people into a small space, Americans are the masters of macro-culture. We want everything in abundance, from our cars to our homes to our meals. Americans don't want to hear that they need to downsize or scale back. Recently, an American car manufacturer planned a new version of one of their classic cars that was five inches smaller. This was a mistake. While five inches is a minimal difference, five inches *larger* would send a much more potent message. We have never taken the notion of cutting back well. How many of us listen to our doctors when they tell us to eat smaller portions? How many of us muse longingly about living in a smaller house?

Another fascinating thing about America, though, is that within these vast spaces one can find both tremendous diversity and unity. On that drive across the country, the landscape changes dramatically, from the rocky coast of Maine to the concrete magnificence of New York City to the wide plains of the Midwest to the awesome expanse of the Grand Canyon to the soaring redwoods of Northern California. Local flavor changes with equal dynamism. The seafood shack in New England becomes the barbecue joint in North Carolina, the steakhouse in Omaha, the red-hot stand in Chicago, and the vegetarian café in San Francisco. Yet you could stay at a Holiday Inn every night of that drive, walking through the same lobby in Scranton that you'll walk through in Sacramento, and you can grab a grande skim latte the next morning at the local Starbucks before you head off to your next destination. "*E pluribus unum*"—"From the many, one"—is a truly fitting motto for this culture.

This sense of newness, size, diversity, and unity forms a very strong imprint on Americans. Our symbols are eagles gliding in midair, a huge statue of a woman welcoming visitors to our shores, a flag being raised on top of the ruins of a devastated building. These symbols form for us a very strong image of who we are meant to be. When I held discovery sessions to learn the Code for America, I received third-hour stories filled with powerful and poignant imagery.

My most powerful memory of America was seeing the astronauts plant an American flag on the moon. I never felt prouder of this country than I felt in that moment. To me, that represented everything great about us—everything we should be trying to achieve.—*a fifty-one-year-old man*

My first memory of America was going to the Lincoln Memorial when I was a little kid. We'd been on vacation in Washington for a couple of days at this point and we'd seen many things, but that image of Abraham Lincoln sitting there made a huge impression on me. My mother told me that Lincoln "freed the slaves." I had no idea what that meant at the time, but it sounded like something big, and that meant a lot to me. It gave me some idea about what Americans were supposed to do.—*a twenty-six-year-old man*

My son's soccer team held a candlelight vigil the Friday after 9/11. Lots of us were crying, including many of the kids, but as

I saw the lights flickering in these boys' eyes, I saw hope. They were confused and maybe even a little frightened, but I never believed for a second that they would be intimidated. They were the future of America and they had so much to accomplish in their lives.—*a forty-year-old woman*

My most powerful memory of America came at the end of the movie *Planet of the Apes* (the original, not the remake). When I saw the Statue of Liberty buried in the sand, I felt incredibly sad. At the same time, though, I told myself that something like this movie would never happen, that America would always live on because Americans had the vision to keep it alive.—*a forty-seven-year-old man*

My father may have been the most patriotic person who ever lived. He came here when he was a young boy and he believed that the opportunities he got here were greater than he would have gotten anywhere else. Every night at bedtime, he told us stories about America and about great Americans. I went to sleep with these visions of greatness dancing in my head. I'd like to believe I've passed that sense of patriotism down to my children and my grandchildren.—*a sixty-two-year-old woman*

The range of these messages was very striking: from the simplicity of a father's bedtime stories to the innocence of a child learning about Lincoln for the first time; from the sadness and resolve of seeing the image of a fallen icon or youngsters bearing up under tragedy to the pride of witnessing our flag flying on alien soil. What did not change, though, was the energy of the stories. The use of phrases like "everything we should be trying to achieve," "it sounded big and that meant a lot to me," "I saw hope," "keep it alive," and "greatness dancing in my head" suggested a mythological dimension, a hyperreality that came to mind when Americans thought about America.

The American Culture Code for America is DREAM

Dreams have driven this culture from its earliest days. The dream of explorers discovering the New World. The dream of pioneers opening the West. The dream of the Founding Fathers imagining a new form of union. The dream of entrepreneurs forging the Industrial Revolution. The dream of immigrants coming to a land of hope. The dream of a new group of explorers landing safely on the moon. Our Constitution is the expression of a dream for a better society. We created Hollywood and Disneyland and the Internet to project our dreams out into the world. We are the product of dreams and we are the makers of dreams.

Discovering this Code puts many of the other Codes in this book into context. We see love as false expectations because we dream of romances that can last a lifetime. We see beauty as man's salvation because we dream that we can truly make a difference in someone's life. We see fat as checking out because we chase dreams so hard that they sometimes overwhelm us. We see health as movement because we dream of a life without limits. We think of work as who we are because we dream that we have a contribution to make and that we can become tremendously successful at our chosen professions. We see shopping as reconnecting with life because we dream of our place in a bigger world. We see money as proof, and luxury as military stripes, because money and luxury make visible our dreams of our best selves. We see the American president as Moses because we dream that someone can lead us to an even better America.

Our notion of abundance is a dream: it is the dream of limitless opportunity that we believe is synonymous with being American. Our need for constant movement is the expression of a dream in which we can always do more, always create and accomplish. Even our cultural adolescence is a dream: we want to believe we are forever young and that we never truly have to grow up.

We've built our culture on dreamlike stories that, amazingly, are true. An undertrained militia defeats the most powerful army in the world to give us our freedom. A child is born into slavery and goes on to become one of the world's greatest inventors. Two brothers battle with the laws of physics and give man wings. A woman refuses to be relegated to the back of the bus and touches off a social revolution. A team of kids comes from nowhere to win an Olympic gold medal against all odds. A young man develops a great idea in his garage and becomes the wealthiest person on the planet.

We have become the most powerful, most influential culture in the world because we believe in the power of dreams. Optimism is not only absolutely on Code, it is essential to keeping our culture vibrant. We do the "impossible" because we believe it is our destiny. In fact, the times when America has faltered as a culture have been the times when it has allowed pessimism to become a prevalent force. The Great Depression was this culture's longest period of national despair, and it went on so long because we forgot that we were capable of doing the impossible and getting ourselves out of it. In the mid to late 1970s, we again bowed to pessimism, as high rates of unemployment, an oil crisis, and a harrowing hostage situation led us to think less of ourselves. In both cases, dreams raised us back up—the dream of the New Deal and the dream of the new America of the Reagan administration.

Pessimism is off Code in America, as is self-hatred. We must always keep in mind that mistakes are valuable to us because we learn from them and become stronger as a result. When we have a down period, we must always keep in mind that we have historically followed these with long stretches of growth and prosperity. Our European friends have predicted the "end" of America dozens of times, but the end has never even come close to happening. One of our favorite icons is the

Comeback Kid. We love people who fail and then rise up again (as in Bill Clinton's comeback after the Lewinsky scandal and Martha Stewart's comeback from imprisonment) because it is such a strong cultural trait. The way New York City (and the entire country, really) bounced back after 9/11 is truly inspiring and precisely on Code.

Few have had any lasting success selling pessimism in America. Hollywood occasionally flirts with dark, European-style movies, but its blockbusters consistently reflect magic and dreams. Unabashed creativity and happy endings are right on Code. Some books critical of America and the American culture have hit American best-seller lists over the years, but the books that endure offer promise and hope. Even the negative campaigning that currently typifies politics has an optimistic undertone. It has a strong reptilian character that tells us "Everything will be fine as long as you vote for me."

OUR PRIMARY MISSION: KEEPING THE DREAM ALIVE

Remaining on Code means supporting our dreams and our dreamers. We want to encourage people to have big ideas, to take risks, and to learn from their mistakes. We want to promote reinvention and starting over. It is entirely on Code for people to change careers, locales, or living situations as long as they genuinely believe that doing so gives them a chance to grow. We want our politicians to give us visions of a better tomorrow. We want our entertainers to stir our imaginations. We want our corporations to show us how their products improve our conditions. We want our teachers to inspire creativity. We want our clergy to give us hope and guidance in living fulfilling lives. We want our media to show us what others are doing to contribute to the world.

America should never shut the door to exploration and discovery. As impractical as it seems, the space program is right on Code. The American journey to the moon is a landmark in the history of our culture and the history of the world. We were the first people ever to free ourselves from this planet and go to another one. Rather than closing down the space program because it costs too much and accomplishes too little, we should set grander goals. If going to Mars seems nearly impossible, it will be that much more satisfying to get there. Dreams are priceless.

America can never stop welcoming immigrants because to do so would be to quash one of our most enduring dreams. Safeguards are, of course, necessary, but the new blood that comes with immigration keeps the dream of America alive for all of us. If someone wants to come here and embrace our culture, that makes our culture stronger and at the same time reminds us why America is unique.

We can also never stop promoting ourselves and our philosophy to the rest of the world. While we must always respect the cultures of others and understand that we cannot make a culture contravene its own Code, sharing the optimism and dreams of America benefits the entire world. Isolationism and protectionism are not only foolhardy in an increasingly global economy, but also utterly off Code. It is America's mission to provide dreams to humanity. Not by forcing our ideology down anyone's throat, but by sharing our vision in our films, our books, our products and inventions, our acts of charity, and our efforts in bringing aid to underdeveloped nations.

YOUR PRESCRIPTION IS READY

The Culture Code offers the benefit of great new freedom gained from understanding why you act the way you do. It gives you a new set of glasses with which you can see the world in a new way. We are all individuals, and each of us has a complex set of motivations, inspirations, and guiding principles—a personal Code, if you will. However, seeing how we think *as a culture,* how we behave as a group in predictable patterns based on the survival kit we received at birth as

Americans, or English, or French, enables us to navigate our world with a vision we've heretofore lacked.

As we close, consider one additional freedom that comes to Americans via the cultural unconscious. That is the freedom to dream, to eschew cynicism and pessimism, and to allow yourself to imagine the boldest things for yourself and your world.

For Americans, nothing is more on Code.

AFTERWORD

Welcome to My Village: The Culture Code and Globalization

A number of years ago, I did some work with Jack Daniel's to help them extend their brand in the global market. This came at a time when there was a dramatic rise in anti-American sentiment throughout the world and the company was seriously concerned that they would suffer internationally because of this. After all, their main product—sour mash whiskey—is one closely associated with American culture since this kind of whiskey is significantly different from the kinds made in other countries. Imagine, for instance, how scotch producers might feel if there were a sudden wave of negative sentiment toward Scotland (or, in fact, what French winemakers faced from a pocket of American consumers after French opposition to the war in Iraq).

When we went out to explore what Jack Daniel's meant around the world, though, we learned something completely unexpected. In conversation after conversation, participants in different countries talked about their anger with and confusion over America—but expressed their fascination with and affection for Jack Daniel's. They loved the image the product projected of a whiskey distilled the same way in a small Southern town for more than a hundred years. To them it suggested visions of small-town folks putting everything they had into their craft and creating something special.

Simply put, the participants hated America, but they loved Jack

Daniel's. Why? Because in their minds, Jack Daniel's wasn't from America—it was from Tennessee.

What we uncovered here is especially telling at a time when it's more important than ever for brands to have a global presence while at the same time contending with the instability of world opinion. For a brand to thrive in the global marketplace, it needs to promote its village of origin.

This might seem somewhat counterintuitive. Logic would seem to suggest that if the world were becoming flatter, then brands would succeed by developing a global image tailored to that flat world. The thinking in many corporations is that a brand needs to find its place around the globe by targeting its message to a particular market (in essence, redefining itself in every region of the world) or by creating a one-size-fits-all global stance that appeals to everyone.

Some of this, of course, is true. Remember a few of the discoveries we made earlier in this book. Nestlé needed to redefine their brand in order to bring instant coffee to the Japanese. Jeep needed to pitch their Wrangler somewhat differently in Europe than they did in the United States. But remember as well one of the primary lessons of international marketing when seen through the glasses of the Culture Code—it is essential that a brand or product maintain a sense of where it comes from when it goes out into the world. Yes, the Wrangler might be a "horse" in the United States and a "liberator" in Germany, but it is always a distinctively American car.

Jack Daniel's is a hugely successful international brand, and a look at their website shows how effectively they've managed to connect their product to their village of origin everywhere in the world. Their home page invites browsers to enter via a list of countries and languages. If you're from Mozambique, you can read the site in Portuguese and if you're from Honduras, you can get it in Spanish—but the overarching message is consistent in every language. When you come to visit the Jack Daniel's site, you come to visit their village of origin. You can tour the Lynchburg, Tennessee, distillery, learn the

history of the distinctive Jack Daniel's bottle, and even read a brief bi-
ography of Jack Daniel himself. Yes, you might discover a series of
pub concerts the company sponsors in England, or a high-tech
screensaver available to Indian customers—items designed to promote the product somewhat differently in different markets—but the
village of origin is always front and center.

How a brand defines its village of origin varies from case to case.
Sometimes the village is actually a village, as it is with Lynchburg. In
other cases, a country serves as the "village." Consider the tremendously successful global re-launch of the Mini Cooper. Throughout
the world—from Chile to Estonia—Mini presents itself as the arche-
typal British touring vehicle. It doesn't matter that German car manufacturer BMW owns Mini (any more than it matters that Jeep is now
owned by Daimler Chrysler). The Mini Cooper is a modernized version of the legendary car created by the British Motor Corporation
and it broadcasts its "British-ness" loudly. Ads around the world sell
the Mini Cooper as a conspicuously British vehicle, harkening back to
the car's status as a '60s pop icon. Again, the pitch changes slightly
from market to market—Mini emphasizes the car's raciness in Italy
and the fun nature of the driving experience in Canada—but they always promote it as a British car. In fact, you can find Mini Coopers all
over the world with a representation of the British flag painted on
their roofs. In Mini's case, the village of origin is England, touching
on the once-proud tradition of British car manufacturing that is now
all but lost but which still resonates throughout the world.

You can see yet another successful example of this in the way some
Australian vineyards have chosen to sell their wines to the world. Australian wine is still something of an upstart in the international market.
While some truly fine Australian winemakers have gained a place
among connoisseurs everywhere, mass marketing in the face of behe-
moths from France, Italy, and America is a challenge for most Australian vineyards. To meet this challenge, some very successful brands
have turned to selling village of origin, reflecting the perception of

Australia as untamed, casual, and irreverent—the land that gave us Crocodile Dundee and Steve Irwin. Among the most popular Australian labels (according to www.winelibrary.com) are Woop Woop Shiraz, Yellowtail Chardonnay (with the image of a bounding kangaroo on its label), and Yard Dog White. In fact, the third most popular Australian wine on the Wine Library site is Cheeky Chick Pecker's Blend. These wines boldly make a place for themselves in a tremendously competitive world by selling where they come from—and the attitude associated with that place—at least as aggressively as what they are.

The village of origin can create an indelible connection to a brand. A product becomes so closely associated with the village that it is nearly impossible to market it any other way. Kobe beef comes from Wagyu cattle, raised in a Japanese region of which Kobe is the capital. American ranchers have found little success in their attempts to market Wagyu beef as a premium brand. However, the same beef marketed as "Kobe-style" beef has more resonance with American foodies. Similarly, a number of years ago, winemakers made an aggressive effort to market wine from a grape varietal known as Sangiovese. It failed to gain traction. Why? Because Chianti (a wine made primarily from Sangiovese grapes) is such a powerfully imprinted village of origin that the wines made from Sangiovese grapes are inextricably tied to the region. The "Chianti Classico" designation is one of the most intensely protected and most heavily promoted "villages" in the entire wine universe, and serious wine drinkers simply don't want to consider Sangiovese wines made elsewhere.

Alternatively, brands that strip the village of origin from their identity soon find they have no mark of distinction at all. While BMW has done a masterful job of keeping the Mini British, Ford has done an awful job with the Jaguar. They moved it to America and redesigned many models to resemble Lincolns so they could build the cars on Lincoln production lines. The upshot? Most Jaguars no longer look like Jaguars. Instead, they look like generic American sedans. They've lost the image of their village of origin and, as sales indicate, they've lost their place in the imaginations of luxury car buyers. A corollary to this is that consumers don't want "global" brands. Consumers associate with a brand when that brand presents itself as something unique. When a product attempts to reconfigure its image to be everything to all cultures, it gives up its uniqueness in an effort to be ultra-accessible. Brands that eschew village of origin to adopt an international personality tend to lose identity as quickly as those that strip village of origin from their marketing message.

To me, the reason for this connects directly to the discoveries I've made uncovering cultural Codes. Cultures perceive globalization as a direct attack on their survival. If the world becomes truly flat and we all exist under one huge planet-wide culture, then we lose the individual cultural identities that have defined us. When brands extend themselves into the global market by championing their villages of origin, they accomplish two tasks at once: they perpetuate their own culture and they celebrate everyone's cultural identity. When Jack Daniel's emphasizes its history in Lynchburg, Tennessee, it defines itself for the world (and, in this case, however unwittingly, insulates itself from anti-Americanism). In addition, though, by embracing its culture, it sends the message that all cultures should do the same. The people who come to the Jack Daniel's website from Honduras receive the unconscious message that cultural differences help distinguish us and that all cultures have a place on the world stage.

The other thing that happens when a brand emphasizes its village of origin is that it transcends time. Jack Daniel's of Lynchburg, Tennessee, connects to a place, and places have a solidity that transcends trend and fashion. Giorgio Armani clothing connects to the eternity of Rome. Marlboro cigarettes connect to the forever nature of the American West. Raymond Weil watches connect to the perpetuity of Geneva. When one associates a brand with the place that gave birth to that brand, the brand becomes an essential part of the landscape. And while landscapes evolve over time, time does not diminish them.

I strongly believe the conversation about culture is a more meaningful and vital conversation now than it has ever been before. The world is connected in ways that it has never been. Borders mean less than they ever have. We all understand that. However, just because we understand it doesn't mean we embrace it. Many people resist globalization because they feel that globalization tears their roots out from under them. They believe that being part of the world community will make them less themselves. (In fact, this would be true. As we've discussed throughout this book, culture has a significant role in showing us who we are. Without a culture to call our own, we'd be profoundly diminished.) Governments can't help us make sense of this. Ideology weighs governments down so much that they can't realistically show us how to navigate through the flattening of the world.

However, commerce can. Understanding that brands stand a far greater chance of succeeding globally when they emphasize their unique heritage (consider Starbucks, Mercedes, Sony, or any number of others) illuminates a fundamental link between culture and viability on the world stage. When a brand identifies itself with its culture, it underscores that culture's contribution to the world. These contributions—and the unspoken invitation to all cultures to contribute what they do best—make the concept of globalization not only palatable but also enviable.

A brand is more than a name or a product. A successful brand is an icon, a powerful expression of a cultural archetype. Therefore, brand managers are not just in charge of reinvesting in the emotional bank account of their brand, but are also in charge of a more important mission: to perpetuate the elements of character of a culture and therefore maintain cultural diversity in the world. In many ways, they are in charge of the Culture Code, in charge of communicating to the global community the power and fascination of culture.

As we all become citizens of this global community, each of us—like each brand—should remember to embrace our village of origin.

ACKNOWLEDGMENTS

A book is like a child . . . with many unknown parents. I might be the known one, but I would like to acknowledge my debt to all who supported my work, encouraged my passion, and gave me hope when I most needed it.

First, of course, are my two sons, Lorenzo and Dorian. Lorenzo is French and was born in Paris. Dorian is American and was born in L.A. They are living examples of the Culture Code!

Second is the one who shared the front line, digging into the collective unconscious, doing the planning and the thinking, and finally the writing. Lou Aronica is definitely more than a writer, he is a thinker and now my American brother in arms.

All this work could not have been accomplished without the internal support and encouragement I got from many of today's CEOs, presidents, and chairmen of major corporations. Special thanks go to A. G. Lafley (Procter & Gamble), Jeff Immelt (GE), Bob Lutz (Chrysler and then GM), Horst Schulze (former president of Ritz-Carlton), Gary Kusumi (GMAC), and John Demsey (Estée Lauder). Against all odds and despite traditional thinkers on their team, they trusted me. Together we have done remarkable work in breaking the Culture Code.

After thirty years of digging into the core of the collective uncon-scious, I want to thank the publisher who understood there were di-amonds to be found. Special thanks to everyone at Doubleday Broadway and especially to my editor, Kris Puopolo, whose sugges-tions were always a creative stimulation and inspired me to identify better and more direct ways to communicate the depth of different things.

My agent Peter Miller is my "favorite lion" (this is his Code), and he has been fighting for this book like a lion. Scott Hoffman also knows how to roar, and his assistance has been invaluable.

ABOUT THE AUTHOR

Dr. Clotaire Rapaille is the chairman of Archetype Discoveries Worldwide and has used this decoding approach for thirty years. He is the personal adviser to ten high-ranking CEOs and is kept on retainer by fifty Fortune 100 companies. He has been profiled in many national media outlets, including *60 Minutes II* and on the front page of the *New York Times* Sunday Styles section. He lives in Tuxedo Park, New York.